Market Institutions, Transaction Costs, and Social Capital in the Ethiopian Grain Market

Eleni Z. Gabre-Madhin

RESEARCH REPORT 124

INTERNATIONAL FOOD POLICY RESEARCH INSTITUTE
WASHINGTON, D.C.

Library of Congress Cataloging-in-Publication Data

Gabre-Madhin, Eleni Zaude.
Market institutions, transaction costs, and social capital in the Ethiopian grain market / Eleni Z. Gabre-Madhin.
p. cm. — (Research report ; 124)
Includes bibliographical references.
ISBN 0-89629-126-X
1. Grain trade—Ethiopia. 2. Grain—Ethiopia—Marketing. 3. Transaction costs. 4. Institutional economics. I. Title. II. Research report (International Food Policy Research Institute) ; 124.

HD9047.E82 G33 2001
381′.4131′0963—dc21 2001055539

Contents

Tables

Figures

Foreword

In the wake of the market reforms sweeping the developing world, a consensus is emerging that these reforms have been only partially successful in sub-Saharan Africa. Although market liberalization has resulted in significant market efficiency gains, reform has failed to enhance market development in terms of increased trader investment, increased market volume and value added, and the emergence of mechanisms to transfer producer risk. Ethiopia, like other liberalizing countries, faces the challenge of learning how to foster market institutions that enhance private market development.

The Ethiopian government fully liberalized the grain market in March 1990, lifting all restrictions on private inter-regional trade flows, removing official pricing and quotas, and eliminating the monopoly status of the marketing board. Despite reform, only 28 percent of total cereals production reaches the market and only 18 percent passes through the marketing chain, suggesting considerable scope for expanding the volume of the grain market. Private sector trade is constrained by weak public market information; the lack of a transparent system of grades and standards for grain; the use of verbal, nonstandardized contracts; and weak legal enforcement of contracts. In response, private traders either exchange with partners they know well or engage brokers who act as agents on their behalf.

Using a New Institutional Economics framework, this research report addresses a fundamental aspect of markets: *how* do buyers and sellers find each other and coordinate the transfer of goods? The report quantifies the transaction costs related to search faced by traders in Ethiopia and analyzes the role of brokers in minimizing these transaction costs. The transaction costs of market search are significant in the Ethiopian grain market. Estimated as the opportunity cost of labor time spent searching for a trading partner and the opportunity cost of holding capital fixed during that search, these costs represent one-fifth of all marketing costs. This research report demonstrates that traders minimize their transaction costs of search by using brokers, who enable them to exchange with unknown partners. The report also shows that at the level of the grain economy as a whole, brokers significantly increase the total economic welfare by enabling a more efficient allocation of search effort by traders. Thus, traders with relatively higher search efficiency and lower search costs choose to search on their own, while traders with lower search efficiency and higher search costs choose to use a broker.

There are important policy implications:

- The high search costs facing private traders must be reduced.
- Social capital among traders must be enhanced and expanded in order to increase market volume.

- The specialized function of brokers in the market must be promoted to capitalize on the welfare gains of brokerage.

The findings of this research report are applicable to many developing countries in which high transaction costs present a serious constraint to market performance and governments are concerned with promoting market institutions in order to foster market development in the postreform era.

Per Pinstrup-Andersen
Director General

Acknowledgments

I wish to make special mention of the Ethiopian grain traders and brokers who willingly participated in the survey I conducted with the aid of colleagues. These traders and brokers spent many hours explaining their livelihoods to strangers from whom they could not expect much in return. It is my hope that the insights from this research will be used by policymakers to produce a positive effect in their lives. The success of the survey is due to one person in particular, Million Tafesse, our research supervisor, who showed enthusiasm, dedication, and energy beyond the call of duty, to whom I am deeply grateful. I also thank the team of intelligent and meticulous enumerators, Solomon Alemu, Gebre Bidada, Hayat Abdulahi, and Mesfin Tadesse.

In Ethiopia the research benefited from the institutional support of the Institute of Development Research and the Department of Economics at Addis Ababa University, headed by Professor Johannes Kinfu and the late Ato Makonnen Tadesse. In addition, I thank Dr. Mulat Demeke, Dr. Wolday Amha, Ato Bereket Kebede, and the late Professor Eshetu Chole for providing useful insights during the field research.

I gratefully acknowledge the financial support of the Rockefeller Foundation, the International Food Policy Research Institute, the Institute of International Studies, and the Olin Foundation of Law and Economics at Stanford University. I am grateful to Dr. Marcel Fafchamps and Dr. Jeffrey Williams at Stanford University for their invaluable advice.

I also owe special thanks to Dr. Agnes Quisumbing at IFPRI for her insightful review of the research report manuscript and to participants in seminars held at IFPRI, the World Bank, USAID-Ethiopia, and the Ministry of Economic Development and Cooperation in Ethiopia. The research also benefited immensely from careful external reviews by Dr. Chris Barrett and Dr. Thomas Jayne. Finally, I thank Diana Flores for her administrative support and Dr. Mark Rosegrant for coordinating the review of this report.

Summary

The Ethiopian government liberalized the grain market in March 1990, lifting all restrictions on private inter-regional trade, removing official pricing and quotas, and eliminating the monopoly status of the marketing board. While market reform has succeeded in reducing marketing margins and improving market integration, the market remains "efficient but poor" in that market development is relatively limited. Reform has *not* led to contractual arrangements to transfer risk, increased impersonal exchange, value added beyond transport, and trader investment. Despite reform, only 28 percent of total cereals production reaches the market and only 18 percent passes through the marketing chain, suggesting considerable scope for expanding the grain market, in terms of volume as well as value added. Several studies have addressed the speed and extent of price transmission in the postreform period in Ethiopia, but the role of market institutions in supporting exchange and the importance of transaction costs and social capital have been given relatively little attention. This report examines a fundamental aspect of market behavior: *how* do buyers and sellers find each other and coordinate the transfer of goods?

To date, little quantitative analysis has been undertaken on transaction costs and institutions, partly because of the difficulty of measuring these costs. This study redresses this gap, using primary data collected on wholesalers and brokers in 1996. Using the New Institutional Economics framework, this study sets forth an empirical analysis of the transaction costs related to search faced by traders in Ethiopia, traders' microeconomic behavior in the market, and the role of brokers who act as intermediaries on behalf of traders.

The analysis of microeconomic trader behavior reveals that Ethiopian grain wholesalers are generally small-scale, personalized enterprises. Traders' arbitrage activity is mainly limited to transport, with an average transported distance of 200 kilometers. Traders are quite competitive in that physical marketing costs related to transport, handling, and other marketing activities represent 83 percent of gross margins, and traders' net margins are less than 5 percent of the sale price.

Weak public market information, the lack of grain standardization, the oral nature of contracts, and limited legal enforcement of contracts increase the risk of commitment failure. In response, traders either choose partners they know well or engage a broker. The presence of brokers facilitates anonymous exchange between traders. However, while 85 percent of traders use brokers regularly, they do so for only a quarter of their total transactions and 33 to 55 percent of their long-distance transactions.

A closer investigation of the norms and rules underlying relations between brokers and traders reveals that relationships are generally long-term, exclusive, and not based on ethnic ties, with only 26 percent of traders of the same ethnicity as their brokers. Brokers and traders avoid conflict through such norms as the specialization of brokers by region and a fixed flat-rate fee, and by the fact that a large number of traders in a given market use the services of the same broker.

Traders are constrained by the opportunity costs of search labor and of holding capital fixed during search. Trader-specific transaction costs of search labor time and of holding working capital during search are estimated as shadow costs from traders' profit functions, using instrumental variable estimation to avoid simultaneity bias. The transaction costs of search are significant, representing 19 percent of total marketing and transaction costs, and are higher in the deficit markets, possibly because of the greater risk of commitment failure in purchasing grain of unknown quality.

Social capital, measured by the network of trading contacts available to each trader, is important in enabling traders to find trading partners more readily. Although traders invest in contacts in distant markets as well as in regular local trading partners, fewer than one-third of trading networks are based on a common ethnic identity.

Economic analysis is used to test whether traders are individually rational in using brokers to minimize their transaction costs of search, based on a two-tiered choice of location of trade and use of broker. Tobit estimation confirms traders' rationality in that the use of brokers is significantly and positively related to both types of search costs and inversely related to their social capital.

An optimal search intensity model is constructed to address whether the institution of brokers increases global efficiency for the market as a whole. The presence of brokers partly internalizes the positive spillovers of individual search behavior through strategic interaction between the market participants, who base their search decisions on conjectures about other traders' decisions to use a broker. With brokers, traders with relatively higher search efficiency and lower search costs choose to search on their own while traders with low search efficiency and high search costs use a broker. Numerical estimation of this model demonstrates that the presence of brokers increases total welfare by 60 percent. Traders with relatively high search efficiency have small welfare losses, while relatively inefficient traders have large welfare gains from using brokers.

This study demonstrates how, in the context of Ethiopia's weak marketing environment, the brokerage institution minimizes transaction costs and facilitates exchange. However, it also reveals that this institution plays a limited role in that traders continue to rely on personalized trade for a significant share of their transactions, even in distant markets.

Three areas for policy intervention emerge from the study findings. The first is how to address the constraints in the marketing environment that lead to high search costs. The second is how to reduce the dominance of personalized exchange, which limits the scope of the market and contributes to a reduced capacity to respond effectively to market signals. The third is how to capitalize on the welfare gains of brokerage by increasing the share of marketed grain handled by brokers.

This research yields insights for other countries. First, policymakers must directly address search as a key market issue that fundamentally influences market dynamics. Second, transaction costs cannot be assumed to be uniform across market participants. Heterogeneity in individual transaction costs leads to different behaviors and different types of institutions in the market.

CHAPTER 1

Introduction

> In fact, the costs of transacting are the key to the performance of economies. There have always been gains from trade . . . but so too have there been obstacles to realizing these gains. If transport costs were the only obstacle, then we would observe through history an inverse relationship between transport costs, on the one hand, and trade and exchange and the well-being of societies on the other.
>
> —Douglass North, 1989

Over the past two decades, recognition of the critical role of markets in economic development has prompted sweeping market reforms across a number of developing countries.[1] The Ethiopian grain economy underwent a dramatic market reform in March 1990, when the government lifted, overnight, all restrictions on private trade, following a period of 15 years in which the state had exercised tight control over prices and interregional movements of grain (Lirenso 1993). The liberalization of the Ethiopian grain market spelled the rejection of state-controlled channels, the return of private traders dispossessed of their trade during the socialist regime, and the restoration of age-old trading relationships and market networks (Dadi, Negassa, and Franzel 1992; Amha 1994; Gebremeskel, Jayne, and Shaffer 1998).

In the postreform period, recent studies have pointed to continued market segmentation, price volatility, and the lack of trader investment in Ethiopia (Kuawab Business Consultants 1994; Dercon 1995; Negassa and Jayne 1997). In spite of the large amount of literature on market performance following market reforms in sub-Saharan Africa, relatively little attention has been given to the role of market institutions in supporting exchange (Barrett 1997; Bryceson 1993; Fafchamps 1996b; Gebremeskel, Jayne, and Shaffer 1998).[2] Even less has been given to understanding how particular institutions effectively reduce transaction costs. Yet it is increasingly recognized that the formulation of market-enhancing policy requires a clearer understanding of transaction costs, institutional marketing arrangements, and microeconomic trader behavior (Palaskas and Harriss-White 1993; Dercon 1995).

[1] Market reform includes, but is not limited to, policies aimed at allowing private sector participation in exchange, removing government trading monopolies, lowering or eliminating tax or licensing restrictions, and eliminating official price setting.

[2] See Kherallah et al. (2000) for a synthesis of findings on market reform in Sub-Saharan Africa.

To date, very little quantitative analysis has been undertaken on transaction costs and institutions, partly due to the difficulty of measuring these costs. This study aims to redress this gap through an empirical analysis of the nature and extent of the transaction costs faced by traders in Ethiopia, traders' social capital and microeconomic behavior in the market, and the role of the institution of brokers as a means of minimizing transaction costs. Using primary data collected on wholesalers and brokers in 1996, the study analyzes the microeconomic behavior of traders in terms of their operations and arbitrage in the market. Using the New Institutional Economics framework, it undertakes an institutional analysis of the role and functions of brokers and the norms governing the relations between traders and brokers. The study also estimates traders' transaction costs related to market search and traders' social capital, and it econometrically tests the individual rationality of traders' choices to use brokers as a means of minimizing their transaction costs. Finally, the study develops a numerical model to be used to evaluate the equilibrium effects of the brokerage institution on traders' search behavior and the distribution of welfare gains and losses from the presence of brokers. This report presents a comprehensive analysis of a key market institution in Ethiopia and the role of this institution in reducing transaction costs. The results provide important policy insights on how to facilitate market exchange and promote market development in the wake of liberalization.

The Institution of Brokers in Ethiopia

Why Brokers Exist

Ethiopian grain traders face three major constraints that increase their transaction costs of participating in the grain market. First, traders do not benefit from a system of grain standardization and inspection that would enable them to place orders with long-distance partners for guaranteed qualities and quantities of grain. Instead they must be physically present at the time of transaction in order to visually inspect the grain that is being exchanged. Second, grain traders have very limited recourse to legal means for enforcing contracts. Thus, they trade only with partners whom they know well and trust in order to avoid the high costs of payment delinquency or reneging on the terms of the contract. Third, traders do not have access to a public market information system that enables them to know prices and flows in markets outside of their own. This limits traders' ability to deliver grain to unknown markets or to set contracts to go into effect at a future point in time, thus limiting their scope of spatial or temporal arbitrage.

These market constraints result in high transaction costs for partner search, information, and enforcement for Ethiopian grain traders. In order to reduce these costs, traders engage the services of grain brokers, known as delala, who act as intermediaries on their behalf. The majority of Ethiopia's grain traders, 85 percent, regularly use these intermediaries to conduct their long-distance transactions. Brokers, operating as commission agents, provide the service of matching regional buyers and sellers, as well as handling and inspecting shipments of grain and providing market information to their clients. Brokers have a distinct identity in the market because they do not take market positions themselves, but only act on behalf of traders. There are approximately 40 established brokers in the central market of Addis Ababa, compared to a total of 2,500 wholesalers in the country. These brokers handle roughly 16 percent of the total marketed surplus. Due to their central position, brokers are keenly aware of prices and flows in the market, and their presence enables the Addis Ababa market to function as a clearinghouse for grain in Ethiopia.

Historical and Comparative Perspectives

In addition to the well-known function of brokers in organized commodity exchanges and in housing and labor markets in industrialized countries, there is evidence of brokerage in agricultural markets across Africa, as well as in Asia and Latin America. N. W. Thomas (1908) reports historical evidence of brokers throughout northeast Africa and, to a lesser extent, central and western Africa. Historically, brokers appear to have played a major role in the food trade of the western Sudan and are linked to the presence of Hausa traders (Cohen 1969; Meillassoux 1971; Jones 1972). Gilbert (1969) finds evidence of brokers in nearly all studied food markets in northern Nigeria, where brokers, known as *dillali,* are generally of the dominant ethnic group. Hill (1966) documents the activities of "landlord-brokers" in food markets in the Kumasi market of Ghana, where their role is similar to that of *logeurs* in Mali (Amselle 1969).

Writing of Asia, Lele (1971) describes the role in the Indian foodgrain market of commission agents, known as *adatya* in Mahareshtra or *dalal* in Hindustani, who operate in a manner closely resembling that of Ethiopian brokers. Scott (1985) documents the existence in the Cañete Valley of Peru of commission agents who facilitate exchange between potato producers in the valley and wholesalers in Lima.

Moreover, the same word, derived from the Arabic *dalaal,* is used to describe brokers in Ethiopia (*delala*), India (*dalal*), Nigeria (*dillali*), and Somalia (*dilal*), possibly revealing that the practice of brokerage may have originated in Muslim commercial practices. Pankhurst (1961) documents reports by Marco Polo of "merchants of all nations" trading in 12th-century Ethiopia, while Alvarez (1881) describes the influence of foreign traders including "Moors, from Giada [Jeddah], Morocco, Fez, Tunis, Turks, Greeks, Moors from India, Ormuz, and Cairo" actively trading in Ethiopia in the 13th century.[3] Jackson (1978) also notes the existence of Muslim-dominated trade routes traversing premodern Ethiopia. The overwhelming evidence of brokerage in agricultural markets historically and across countries suggests that this institution has long existed throughout the world as a viable mechanism of promoting trade in the presence of a high rate of commitment failure in constrained marketing environments.

The New Institutional Economics Approach

Transaction Costs

According to the New Institutional Economics (NIE) approach, the unit of analysis is the transaction rather than the price. Exchange itself is costly. Transaction costs, which are distinct from physical marketing costs such as those for transport and storage, arise from the coordination of exchange among market actors. They include the costs of obtaining and processing market information (Hayek 1945; Alchian and Demsetz 1972; Hoff and Stiglitz 1990), negotiating contracts (Coase 1937; Williamson 1985), monitoring agents (Bardhan 1989; Cheung 1968; Eswaran and Kotwal 1985), and enforcing contracts (North 1989; Milgrom, North, and Weingast 1990; Greif 1993; Fafchamps 1996b).

Transaction costs are unique to each market participant, implying that economic actors are not interchangeable. The presence of transaction costs, which are specific to each market actor, implies that there is no single effective market price at which exchange occurs (Sadoulet and de Janvry 1995). Each agent in the market conducts transactions on the basis of his or her specific transaction costs. The implications of transaction costs are that markets are thin or fail if prohibitively high costs prevent exchange.

Institutions to Facilitate Exchange

Institutions are defined as the "rules of the game," both formal rules and informal constraints such as norms, conventions, and codes of conduct that provide the structure for human interaction (North 1990). Institutions emerge to minimize these transaction

[3] Pankhurst (1961), p. 307.

costs and to facilitate market exchange. The evolution from personalized exchange to impersonal or anonymous exchange, supported by legal systems that enforce contracts, is central to the process of growth and development (North and Thomas 1973).

However, following Polanyi (1957), it is widely recognized that market transactions, particularly in developing countries, are often embedded in long-term, personalized relationships (Geertz 1968; Meillassoux 1971; Granovetter 1985; Plattner 1989; Palaskas and Harriss-White 1993). Personalized exchange emerges in response to commitment failure, in which the risk of breach of contract or opportunism is high, resulting from the lack of market information, inadequate regulation, and the absence of legal enforcement mechanisms. Institutions build trust and promote reputation and social capital, such as trade associations, solidarity networks, and groups that enhance ethnic or religious ties, emerge to circumvent commitment failure (Greif 1993; Fafchamps 1996a; Platteau 1994a).

Historically, institutions have emerged in various contexts to facilitate anonymous trade. Historical institutional analysis of premodern trade in medieval Europe by Milgrom, North, and Weingast (1990) shows that an institution known as the Law Merchant enabled impersonal exchange to occur in 12th- and 13th-century Champagne fairs. The Law Merchant enabled trade through a reputation mechanism that stored information about traders' past behavior and sanctioned violators of the commercial code. Greif (1993) views the Maghribi traders' coalition formed in the 11th century as a means of overcoming the commitment problem intrinsic to long-distance trade. Clay (1993) shows that coalitions of long-distance traders in 19th-century Mexican California promoted honest exchange through information sharing and punishing of cheaters. In contrast, Platteau (1994a, 1994b) argues that decentralized arrangements based on reputation are not sufficient to ensure honest behavior and that private and public-order institutions are necessary to create the social conditions necessary for markets to operate. Fafchamps and Minten (1999) demonstrate that the dominant contract enforcement mechanism in liberalized grain markets in Madagascar is trust-based relationships, where trust is established primarily by repeated interaction. The incidence of theft and breach of contract is low, and recourse to the legal system is rare.

Social Capital

Although social scientists have long recognized the role of interpersonal relationships in human interaction (Coleman 1988; Granovetter 1985), the concept of social capital has been little used in economics (Fafchamps and Minten 1999; Barr 1997; Narayan and Pritchett 1996). There are two possible meanings of social capital. The first definition sees social capital as a "stock" of trust and an emotional attachment to a group or society that facilitates the provision of public goods (Fukuyama 1995; Greif 1993; Coleman 1988; Putnam, Leonardi, and Nanetti 1993). The second views social capital as an individual asset that provides private benefits a single individual or firm (Granovetter 1985; Montgomery 1991; Aoki 1984).

Despite the important strides made in the institutional literature, several gaps remain. First, relatively little institutional research has addressed the role of intermediaries in facilitating exchange between anonymous partners. Second, very little attention has been given to a critical transaction cost, the cost of search. That is, little institutional analysis has been undertaken on the process by which economic agents find each other in the market. Third, very few empirical studies have attempted to measure transaction costs quantitatively, partly due to the difficulty of obtaining data on these types of costs. Finally, this literature generally overlooks the implications of the existence of institutions for behavior in equilibrium. Most institutional analyses assume that an institution exists because it minimizes costs, without examining the implications of the presence of the institution for the welfare of the economy.

Study Objectives and Policy Relevance

This study aims to empirically analyze how the institution of brokerage minimizes the transaction costs of search in the Ethiopian grain market. The analysis is based on primary data collected in 1996 in a survey of 169 traders and brokers. The sample population represents roughly 7 percent of the total population of traders in the country during that period. The specific objectives of this report are to address several questions in order to inform policy aimed at facilitating market exchange and promoting market development. These questions are as follows:

1. What is the microeconomic behavior of traders in the market?
2. What is the nature and extent of transaction costs faced by traders?
3. How important are transaction costs relative to physical marketing costs?
4. What functions do brokers play and how does their presence facilitate impersonal exchange?
5. Does the brokerage institution enable traders to reduce their transaction costs?
6. Does the presence of brokers enhance global economic welfare?

The empirical approach taken in this study enables policy analysts to determine how important institutions and transaction costs are to traders' microeconomic behavior and to global welfare. The interaction between market institutions and transaction costs can be used to infer the wider impact of policy measures to reduce these costs. This is a critical first step in understanding how existing market institutions can be promoted or new institutions be designed to improve market performance.

Structure of This Report

Chapter 2 gives a general overview of the grain economy, including the policy environment. The chapter reviews secondary evidence on the impact of market reform on prices, marketing margins, and integration. In addition, it presents background information on grain production and demand, as well as reviewing general features of the grain market, such as seasonality, infrastructure, and the marketing channels. Chapter 3 presents survey data on traders in terms of their individual characteristics and their asset base, as well as a profile of trading businesses. The chapter also explores the spatial pattern of grain flows in the survey year and traders' marketing costs and arbitrage behavior. The chapter serves mainly to provide a backdrop for analysis of the brokerage institution and of transaction costs. Based on original data, Chapter 4 defines the role and functions of brokers. The chapter addresses how brokers reduce commitment failure and promote market exchange. Chapter 5 undertakes a focused institutional analysis of the norms and rules governing agency relations between traders and brokers. Chapter 6 presents the nature and of traders' search costs and social capital, and instrumental variable estimation is used to derive traders' individual transaction costs of search. Chapter 7 explores traders' sequential choice of brokerage to minimize their transaction costs of search using Tobit estimation. Chapter 8 addresses whether brokerage enhances global efficiency at the level of the marketing system. An equilibrium model is constructed in which traders choose an optimal level of search effort to maximize their revenues as a function of their specific transaction costs of search and their social capital. Finally, Chapter 9 considers implications for policy and further research.

CHAPTER 2

The Ethiopian Grain Economy

This chapter reviews secondary evidence regarding the context of grain trade in Ethiopia. The chapter provides background information on the policy environment and the effect of market reform on market price levels, price spreads between markets, and market integration. It also reviews the structure and location of production, as well as of demand, including food security considerations. It then reviews market seasonality, infrastructure, and the structure of the market, including the distribution of traded volumes throughout the marketing channel. Thus, the chapter provides a synthesis of recent research findings on the situation and structure of grain markets in Ethiopia.

The Policy Environment

Between 1976 and 1990 a government-owned enterprise, the Agricultural Marketing Corporation (AMC), strictly controlled grain trade. The AMC administered a highly distorted trade regime in which official prices were set below producer costs. Under the official pricing system, the magnitude of producers' losses varied from 24 percent for wheat to 52 percent for teff (Amha 1994).[4] Marketing policy in this period included the administration of a compulsory delivery system with fixed quotas for all producers. Each farmer was forced to supply a fixed quota of grain for the purpose of feeding the army and certain urban areas. In addition, inter-regional movement of grain by the private sector was severely restricted (Lirenso 1993). Private sector trade was banned entirely in the major grain-producing areas of Gojjam and Arsi, while other regions required that traders supply 50 to 100 percent of their grain turnover to the AMC at below-market prices (Dercon 1995). In urban areas the AMC operated food ration shops for consumers, which further distorted the grain market.

In response to external pressures, a radical and abrupt market reform was enacted literally overnight in 1990, taking the government parastatal as well as private traders by surprise (Fisseha 1994). The following excerpt from the proclamation of March 1990 reveals the extent of the reform: "In the trade sector of the economy, private entrepreneurs will be able to compete with state-run trade enterprises in agriculture or industrial commodities as well as in import-export trade. In the area of trade in grain products in particular, trade exchange

[4] Teff, or *Eragrot teff*, is a grain indigenous to Ethiopia and the primary staple used in the production of *injera*, a widely consumed flat bread.

will henceforth be conducted on the basis of free market pricing while the grain control situation and the quota system will cease. The Agricultural Marketing Corporation (AMC) will enter the free market and operate as a state trade organization." The reform of 1990 resulted in the restoration of private trade and the transformation of the parastatal, renamed the Ethiopian Grain Trade Enterprise, into a buffer stock scheme. The modern warehouses built by the AMC in the monopoly period, numbering 2,200 and with a total storage capacity in excess of 1 million tons, were made available for rental to private entities and relief agencies, although their utilization was only 50 percent in 1992 (Lirenso 1993).

The Impact of Market Reform

The market reform experienced in Ethiopia in the period since 1990 is considered a relatively consistent and internally driven process, generally approved by the international donor community (Jayne, Negassa, and Myers 1998). Therefore, the Ethiopian case presents an interesting opportunity to test the hypothesis that market reform would lead to reduced costs and risks of marketing and would stimulate production. Recent studies have evaluated the impact of reform on the price levels and marketing spreads, as well as the speed of price transmission between markets.

Price Levels, Spreads, and Volatility

A recent study by Jayne, Negassa, and Myers (1998) evaluates the impact of reform on inflation-adjusted grain prices and price spreads among major markets. Using monthly price data on eight markets over nine years (1987 to 1996), the results reveal that average real prices of maize and teff increased after reform for the surplus markets and declined for the deficit markets. Thus, prices in the surplus areas increased in all cases by 16 percent to 46 percent, while prices in deficit areas decreased in four out of six cases by 15 percent to 120 percent. Price variability declined after reform, with the coefficient of variation of monthly prices declining in 8 out of 12 cases (Table 2.1).

Table 2.1 Monthly real prices before and after market reform (Eth. Birr per bag)

	Before reform			After reform			Change		
	Mean	SD	CV (percent)	Mean	SD	CV (percent)	Mean	SD	CV (percent)
Maize									
Surplus market									
Bako	56.81	22.78	40	82.95	31.71	38	26.14	8.93	−2
Shashamane	64.45	27.89	28	91.65	23.31	25	27.20	−3.49	−3
Jimma	76.27	34.10	45	88.68	28.99	33	12.41	−5.11	−12
Deficit market									
Addis Ababa	96.15	12.41	13	108.50	25.21	23	12.35	12.80	10
Dire Dawa	117.76	25.58	22	150.00	23.31	20	32.24	−2.27	−2
Mekele	196.28	54.11	28	146.72	31.71	12	−49.56	−35.94	−16
White teff									
Surplus market									
Bako	134.82	20.22	15	168.50	26.91	16	33.68	6.69	1
Hosaenna	149.61	20.24	14	184.27	25.47	14	34.66	5.23	0
Bahir Dar	158.65	15.56	10	199.68	29.12	15	41.03	13.56	5
Deficit market									
Addis Ababa	256.90	23.21	9	236.26	19.95	8	−20.64	−3.26	−1
Dire Dawa	301.41	33.26	11	285.95	23.77	8	−15.46	−9.49	−2
Mekele	389.99	48.64	12	269.95	14.49	5	−120.04	−34.15	−7

Source: Jayne, Negassa, and Myers 1998.

Table 2.2 Monthly marketing spreads before and after market reform (Eth. Birr per bag)

Market pair	Before reform			After reform			Change		
	Mean	SD	CV	Mean	SD	CV	Mean	SD	CV
Maize									
Addis Ababa–Bako	39.34	19.79	50	25.55	15.25	60	−13.79	−4.54	10
Addis Ababa–Dire Dawa	21.61	15.97	74	41.50	21.10	51	19.89	5.13	−23
Addis Ababa–Jimma	19.87	28.64	146	19.82	14.10	71	−0.05	−14.54	−75
Addis Ababa–Mekele	98.57	51.98	53	41.67	22.69	54	−56.90	−29.29	1
Addis Ababa–Shashamene	31.69	15.71	60	16.85	11.85	70	−14.84	−3.86	20
Mekele–Bako	149.50	52.00	35	63.22	30.12	48	−86.28	−21.88	13
Mekele–Jimma	132.08	51.87	39	56.26	26.65	47	−75.82	−25.22	8
Mekele–Shashamene	130.74	46.50	36	55.42	20.20	36	−75.32	−26.30	0
White teff									
Addis Ababa–Bako	122.08	29.32	24	67.76	21.36	32	−54.32	−7.96	8
Addis Ababa–Bahir Dar	98.25	21.76	22	34.64	21.54	62	−63.61	−0.22	40
Addis Ababa–Dire Dawa	44.51	22.21	50	49.69	18.12	36	5.18	−4.09	−14
Addis Ababa–Hosaenna	111.04	29.53	27	51.98	18.59	36	−59.06	−10.94	9
Addis Ababa–Mekele	115.81	45.28	39	36.49	21.22	58	−79.32	−24.06	19
Dire Dawa–Bako	142.75	32.69	23	83.61	28.15	34	−59.14	−4.54	11
Dire Dawa–Bahir Dar	157.37	35.13	22	101.67	26.39	26	−55.70	−8.74	4
Mekele–Bako	259.38	44.53	17	103.22	33.62	33	−156.16	−10.91	16
Mekele–Bahir Dar	224.23	45.29	20	66.46	31.15	47	−157.77	−14.14	27
Mekele–Hosaenna	239.00	44.04	18	86.81	28.12	32	−152.19	−15.92	14

Source: Jayne, Negassa, and Myers 1998.

Although favorable weather can partially explain shifts in price levels, it cannot explain the simultaneous increase in prices in surplus areas and the decrease in prices in deficit areas. These suggest that market reform has led to a reduction in price spreads (the difference in prices between surplus and deficit areas). Indeed, in 17 of 19 cases viewed by Jayne, Negassa, and Myers, price spreads declined after reform. The decline in spreads was particularly large for teff, on which the former AMC exercised the greatest restrictions. Reasons suggested for the decline in marketing spreads include (1) lower transaction costs resulting from the elimination of smuggling and bribery (Franzel, Colburn, and Degu 1989); (2) the peace dividend of the end of civil war and disrupted trade in the northern regions (Dercon 1995); (3) benefits of not forcing traders to sell at below-market prices, which bid down producer prices and bid up consumer prices; and (4) less uncertainty related to the commercial activities of the former monopoly. Econometric analysis conducted holding rainfall, seasonality, and other exogenous factors constant reveals that the decline in price spreads was associated with liberalization in 16 out 19 cases and was statistically significant in 10 cases (Negassa and Jayne 1997).

However, although mean price spreads declined after reform, the coefficient of variation of price spreads increased in 15 out of 19 cases, suggesting that the mean levels declined more than the decline in the volatility of price spreads (Table 2.2).

Market Integration

The extent to which price changes in one market are associated with price changes in other markets is known as market integration. Using simple correlation coefficients between wholesale prices across markets, Negassa and Jayne (1997) found that changes in wholesale prices were transmitted more rapidly and more fully after liberalization for 17 out of 24 market pairs observed. A follow-up study of vertical integration of prices from producer to retail levels and spatial integration across markets reveals that after

Table 2.3 Short-run integration of markets after reform (f-test results)

Addis Ababa to:	Prereform (7/87–2/90)	Reform (3/90–5/91)	Postreform (5/91–7/93)
Wolliso	3.07*	1.04	0.34
Debre Zeit	1.84	1.61	0.90
Nazareth	1.85	1.35	3.14*
Ambo	2.76*	1.33	1.06
Dire Dawa	2.78*	0.94	2.75*
Kombolcha	2.98*	1.89–	2.22–
Hosaenna	2.72*	3.32**	1.43
Shashamene	1.64	1.21	0.41
Ziway	2.92*	1.88–	1.70

Source: Dercon 1995.

Notes: – = Short-term integration rejected at 10 percent level; * = integration rejected at 5 percent level; ** = integration rejected at 1 percent level.

reform grain markets showed a high degree of integration (Negassa 1998).

Cointegration analysis was undertaken by Dercon (1995) using six years of deflated monthly teff prices for 11 markets to test for the effect of liberalization on short-term and long-term integration. Using the price in Addis Ababa as the reference price, the test results show that an increased number of markets became linked in the short run to the Addis Ababa market after liberalization (Table 2.3). The cointegrating regression also suggested that reforms resulted in reduced margins between producing areas and consuming areas.

Table 2.4 Production and marketable surplus of grains, 1995/96

Type of grain	Annual production (millions of tons)	Percent production marketed	Total marketed quantity (millions of tons)	Percent total marketed quantity
Cereals	8.3	26	2.16	81
Teff	1.9	24	0.45	21
Wheat	1.2	25	0.30	14
Barley	0.7	31	0.22	10
Maize	2.2	25	0.54	25
Sorghum	2.0	12	0.24	11
Pulses	0.8	37	0.31	12
Oilseeds	0.2	71	0.13	5
Other	0.1	52	0.05	2
Total	9.4	28	2.64	100

Source: Calculated from figures found in Central Statistical Authority 1995 and Gebremeskel, Jayne, and Shaffer 1998.

Grain Production and Marketed Surpluses

Grain production in Ethiopia is almost entirely based on rain-fed agriculture and is characterized by a dominant harvest (*meher*) in November and December and a secondary harvest (*belg*) in April and May. Production is carried out by small-scale farmers with limited agricultural technology and low yields and by a small percentage of state farms.

According to the Central Statistical Authority's *meher* and *belg* production estimates, in 1995/96, which was a relatively good crop year, annual production of grain, including cereals, pulses, and oilseeds, was 9.4 million tons, 98.4 percent of which was produced by smallholders and 1.6 percent by state farms. Of the total produced quantity, the proportion of output marketed by farmers and state farms was 27 percent and 80 percent, respectively (Gebremeskel, Jayne, and Shaffer 1998). As shown in Table 2.4, the proportion of total production that is marketed, that is the extent the crop resembles a "cash crop," varies between crops. Thus, a considerably lower proportion of total production of cereals that is marketed (26 percent), compared to pulses (37 percent) and oilseeds (71 percent). At the same time, because cereals production is the bulk of total grain production, the total marketed quantity of cereals represents 81 percent of the total marketed quantity of grains. Among the cereals, maize has the highest share of total marketed surplus (25 percent), followed by teff (21 percent), and wheat (14 percent).

Surplus Production and Deficit Areas

Both grain-surplus areas and the grain-deficit centers in Ethiopia are geographically dispersed (Figure 2.1). The production of teff is concentrated in Gojjam (55 percent), Shewa (28 percent), and Wollega (4 percent). Wheat is produced in Arsi (63 percent)

Figure 2.1 Administrative regions and zones of Ethiopia

Source: United Nations Emergencies Unit for Ethiopia, March 2000 (http://www.sas.epenn,edu/African_Studies/EUE/M_eue.html).
Note: All boundaries are approximate and unofficial.

and Shewa (25 percent). Maize is produced in Shewa (45 percent), Wollega (34 percent), and Gojjam (15 percent).[5] In terms of demand, Kuawab (1994) estimates that the major deficit areas are concentrated in Addis Ababa, where demand is 32 percent of total marketable surplus, Hararghe (18 percent), Sidamo (7 percent), Wollo (6 percent), and Tigray (4 percent). The dispersion of surplus and deficit areas gives rise to significant interregional flows of grain, as the next chapter explores.

Seasonality in Production and Marketing

There is an important seasonal pattern to the production and marketing of cereals in Ethiopia. Due to the rain-fed nature of agriculture, the grain market depends primarily on the major harvest season, the *meher,* which occurs from November through December. In this period there is a flurry of buying on the part of traders, and prices are at their lowest given the large supply that floods the market as farmers seek to sell in order to meet

[5] Kuawab Business Consultants (1994); Lirenso (1993). These statistics are based on 1979–1988 time series by the Central Statistical Authority. Provincial boundaries were redrawn by the Transitional Government in 1992. Gojjam is now separated into Eastern and Western Gojjam in Amhara region; Shewa is separated into two Northern Shewa zones (in Oromiya and Amhara regions) as well as an Eastern and Western Shewa in Oromiya region; and Arsi zone is located in Oromiya region. Wollo is separated into North and South Wollo zones, both in Amhara region. Hararghe is separated into East and West Hararghe zones, both in Oromiya, while the main urban centers, Harar and Dire Dawa, are considered a separate region. Sidamo is located in Oromiya region.

Figure 2.2 Seasonality in grain prices

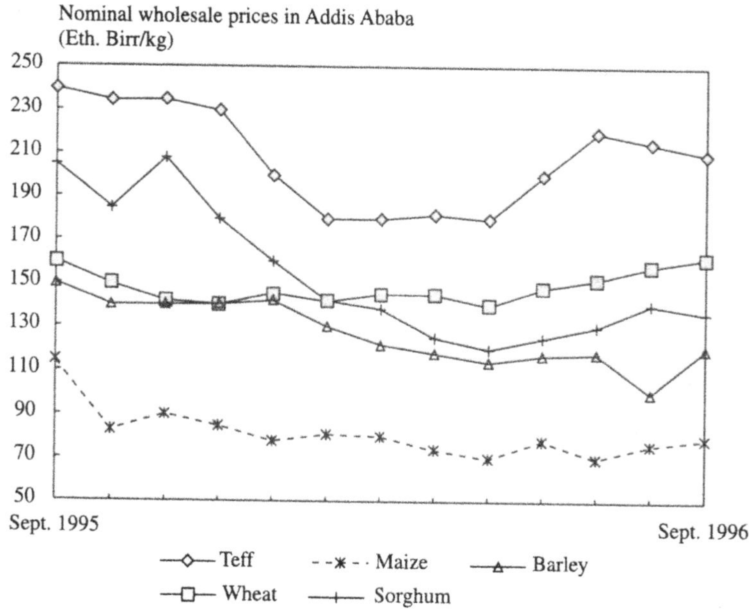

Source: Ethiopian Grain Trade Enterprise 1996.
Notes: Prices given are monthly averages of three weekly observations for the dominant varieties of each type of grain. Eth. Birr 6.35 = US$1 in 1996.

cash obligations related to loan and tax payments, weddings, and food purchases. Thus, 79 percent of the annual sales of farmers occur in the period between January and March (Gebremeskel, Jayne, and Shaffer 1998). Analogously, the main grain-purchasing period for traders is between January and March, during which traders purchase 51 percent of their annual volume. The difference between volumes sold by farmers and those purchased by traders is due to the fact that farmers sell part of their output directly to consumers.

Gebremeskel, Jayne, and Shaffer (1998) report that traders do not provide advance payment, credit, or other price incentives to lock farmers into contracts. Thus, 97 percent of producers indicated that they did not receive preharvest price offers, and fewer than 5 percent of farmers received credit from traders. These results suggest that both forward contracts and interlinked contracts are virtually nonexistent in Ethiopia. This implies that farmers bear the full price risk in marketing their output, without informal mechanisms to lock in prices and without the financial means to withhold sales to mitigate the fall in prices at harvest.

In normal production years prices exhibit a typical seasonal pattern in which, as the new harvest starts to come to the market, prices decline from September, reaching a trough in the period from January to April, when the market is flooded. Although negatively affected by the supplies from the second harvest in April, prices rise in May through August with the approach of the rainy season. As seen in Figure 2.2, this seasonal pattern is similar for most grains with the exception of wheat, the price of which is influenced by food aid deliveries at different times throughout the year.

Grain Demand and Food Security

The most important grains in terms of consumption are teff, wheat, and maize, which together constitute roughly two-thirds of caloric intake in Ethiopia (Lirenso 1993). In urban areas, expenditure on grains constitutes 21 percent of total expenditures (Bereket, Jayne, and Tadesse 1996). Lirenso (1993) estimates that the grain market—dependent population, that is the population depending on the market for all or part of its food supply, was roughly 42 percent of the total population, or 23 million people, in 1992. This figure is for the urban population (15 percent of the total population), the nomadic population (12 percent), and grain-deficit farm households (14 percent).

As seen in Table 2.5, the monthly grain requirements of major urban centers reveals the overwhelming dominance of the Addis Ababa central market, partly explaining why the bulk of surplus grain from around the country flows to this market.

In food security terms, it is generally believed that Ethiopia's total production of grain is not adequate to meet demand, with national production meeting only 65 percent of per capita requirements and a grain deficit of up to 1 million tons in 1994 (Natural Resources Institute 1994). Recent studies, however, indicate otherwise. Results of a major household survey in 1995/96 reveal that some 5 million households, representing 57 percent of total households, are food secure. The remaining 43 percent are food deficit, with a total food gap of 1.4 million metric tons, which is exacerbated by incorrect targeting of food aid (Clay, Molla, and Habtewold 1998).[6] According to Clay, Molla, and Habtewold (1998), sufficient food is available, before food aid imports, to meet the nutritional needs of the entire population. The study indicates that the geographical dispersion of production and the unevenness of trade result in food-secure households' consuming nearly four times more food on average than food-deficit households (with a Gini ratio of food availability of 0.44) and a large segment of the population, the food-deficit population, lacking access to minimum levels of nutrition. These findings emphasize the importance of market distribution in the Ethiopian context and the critical role that markets play in food security.

Table 2.5 Monthly grain requirements of major urban centers, 1992

Urban center	Population	Estimated monthly requirement (thousands of tons)
Addis Ababa	2,111,500	26.4
Dire Dawa	173,588	2.7
Nazareth	131,585	1.8
Harar	109,670	1.7
Mekele	107,671	1.7
Jimma	106,842	1.6

Source: Lirenso 1993.

Market Infrastructure

Transport

Ethiopian transport is composed of road and rail transport. The roads in Ethiopia are built in a radial configuration, with the capital city, Addis Ababa, at the center. This radial structure implies that regional markets cannot trade directly with each other without physically passing through the capital city. So the central market of Addis Ababa has a natural advantage as a national clearinghouse for grain, with sellers bringing grain to the capital and buyers coming to that city to acquire grain. The geographical advantage enjoyed by Addis Ababa at the center of the radial structure of roads is an important feature of the structure of the Ethiopian market, just as, in the United States, the location of Chicago at the confluence of the Illinois River, Lake Michigan, and the continental railroad system played a large part in determining its role as the gateway between the eastern market of New York and the grain-producing American Midwest in the late 19th century.[7]

Road transport in Ethiopia is characterized by high operating costs, a shortage of total truck capacity to meet peak demand, low capacity utilization and load factors, lack of private sector competition, and the dominance of the parastatal Ethiopian Freight Transport Corporation, in addition to poor roads (International Fertilizer Development Centre 1993). Over 80 percent of the rural population has no access to modern transport, while only half of grain markets in major production zones are served by all-weather roads (Lirenso 1993). The majority of traders do not own means of transport; they rely on rented trucks, for which markets are incomplete and linked to the transport of manufactured goods and fertilizer, which constitute the backhaul cargo (International Fertilizer Development Centre 1993). Liberalization of the road freight sector has increased private sector participation to the extent that in 1993 private fleets constituted up to 81 percent and 38 percent of short-haul and long-haul trucks, respectively. In the area of rail transport, a single axis links the neighboring port of Djibouti with Addis Ababa. With the exception of trade into Dire

[6] The food gap is defined as the difference between food available and food need, which is 1,680 kilocalories per person per day.

[7] Cronon (1991) provides a fascinating account of the rise of the Chicago market in the late 19th century as a function of Chicago's geographic advantage, technological advantage (due to the rail and telegraph systems and grain elevators), and institutional advantage (due to the existence of the Board of Trade and established commission merchants).

Dawa, rail transport is not an important means of moving grain in Ethiopia.

Storage

Farm-level storage is carried out by means of primarily traditional basket granaries, while traders generally store grain in warehouses with an average capacity of 100 tons with poor ventilation and dirt floors (Dadi, Negassa, and Franzel 1992). Of the total grain production, some 72 percent is retained for on-farm uses (Gebremeskel, Jayne, and Shaffer 1998). However, weak storage infrastructure leads to potentially high storage losses, with crop vulnerability to damage from weevils, termites, rodents, birds, and moisture. Similarly, although storage capacity has increased since the enactment of market reforms, roughly two-thirds of traders indicate that their storage facilities are still inadequate in terms of availability, capacity, and location, with 19 percent of traders reporting in 1998 that they were unable to obtain rented storage space (Gebremeskel, Jayne, and Shaffer 1998). This inadequacy of storage, combined with the vulnerability of crops to damage, makes traders unwilling to store stocks beyond the minimum turnover period. Modern storage facilities exist in various parts of the country as a legacy of the state-controlled grain-marketing system that was in place prior to reform. There are 2,200 modern warehouses that were used during this period to extract quotas from producers at the fixed prices. These warehouses are located around the countryside, with a capacity of 1 million tons. Since market reform, private traders have access to rented space in these warehouses. However, in 1992 less than one-half of the total capacity was used by private traders (Lirenso 1993).

Information

Access to market information is extremely limited in the Ethiopian grain market. At the producer level, farmers have very little information on prices prevailing even in nearby markets (Amha 1994; Dadi, Negassa, and Franzel 1992). Farmers have indicated that their primary source of market information is the marketplace itself, as well as conversations with neighbors and traders (Grain Market Research Project 1996).

Similarly, grain traders rely on contact with brokers and transporters to obtain market information regarding prices in the Addis Ababa market (Kuawab Business Consultants 1994). Generally traders appear to have very little or no information on imports and food aid shipments, resulting in considerable uncertainty in wheat and maize marketing. Moreover, information on supply, demand, and prices in the central market is unevenly distributed, with only 50 percent of traders indicating that they have access to this information (Gebremeskel, Jayne, and Shaffer 1998). In recent years, efforts have been made by the government to establish a market information system.

Grades and Standards

Finally, grain grading and standardization are limited to visual inspection, at the time of transaction, of the color of the grain, as well as the amount of foreign matter, pest damage, and kernel breakage. Grain is classified on the basis of this quality check and its place of origin. Lack of grain standardization results in prices that are difficult to compare (Dadi, Negassa, and Franzel 1992). The lack of grades and standards is a key factors in the market behavior of traders, subsequent chapters show.

Market Structure

A study of several African markets after reform notes that marketing chains remain relatively short, which is also true of the Ethiopian grain market (Food Studies Group 1992). This is primarily due to the low level of commercial grain processing and the lack of specialization of grain wholesalers, who are often engaged in retail and other types of trade as well. Lirenso (1993) notes that in Ethiopia the marketing chain became more complex after market deregulation, with the selling outlets for farmers increasing threefold, to six outlets, and the supply sources for urban consumers increasing twofold, to four sources. The Ethiopian grain market is structured so that grain moves from producers to rural assemblers, then to regional wholesalers (sellers), then on through central market brokers to regional wholesalers (buyers), then to retailers, and finally to consumers.

Producers

Small-scale farmers produce 95 percent of Ethiopian grain (Kuawab Business Consultants 1994). Grain reaches the market from the farm in four principal ways: by means of direct sales to rural and urban consumers, direct sales to rural assemblers, direct sales to retailers, and direct sales to either regional wholesalers or mills (Gebremeskel, Jayne, and Shaffer, 1998). Farmers transport grain to the nearest regional market themselves, either carrying sacks themselves or using donkeys over relatively short distances of up to 20 kilometers, and they sell directly to wholesalers (Lirenso 1993). Farmers also sell small quantities of grain to rural assemblers known as "farmer-traders," larger-scale farmers who assemble grain from a large number of farmers and transport it to the regional market using horse-driven carts. The role of farmer-traders is widely prevalent and resembles the role of village collectors in peasant markets of rural Indonesia (Hayami and Kawagoe 1993). Farmers also sell grain directly to retailers in regional market towns. Finally, farmers sell directly to wholesalers in the regional market or sell to regional traders who move from village to village, purchasing grain until their trucks are filled.

Rural Assemblers

Assemblers, mainly farmer-traders, buy grain from farmers in rural markets for the purpose of reselling it to consumers or regional wholesalers. Although they typically operate independently, they may also act as agents for wholesalers on a fixed-fee or commission basis (Gebremeskel, Jayne, and Shaffer, 1998).

Regional Wholesalers (Sellers)

At the level of the regional market, wholesalers purchase grain either from farmers or from rural assemblers. They resack the grain and store it for up to 46 days on average. They have four major market outlets; they may sell it in the Addis Ababa central market or in another terminal market through the services of a broker, they may sell it to nearby mills (for wheat), to retailers, or directly to local consumers and restaurants.

Central Market Brokers

Grain brokers are typically located in Addis Ababa, although new market hubs are emerging in Nazareth. Brokers acknowledge receipt of the grain from the regional wholesalers, inspect its quality, determine its market-clearing price, and proceed to sell it on behalf of their clients. Brokers may identify as buyers other traders, flour mills, hotels or restaurants, government agencies, or nongovernmental organizations.

Typically a grain broker representing a seller will interact with a grain broker representing a buyer. If no buyer is found, the grain remains on the truck for up to two days, after which it is off-loaded into the broker's warehouse. The seller bears the off-loading costs as well as additional storage costs charged by the broker. These costs are extremely high compared to the broker's commission fee. Although the broker's fee varies between Eth. Birr 1.00 and Eth. Birr 1.50 per sack, storage costs are Eth. Birr 2.00 per sack for 1 to 30 days and Eth. Birr 2.00 per month thereafter. Due to these high costs, it is only rarely that a shipment is not sold from the seller's truck.

Regional Wholesalers (Buyers)

In deficit areas regional wholesalers, through the services of a broker, purchase grain from regional sellers. Typically the buyer pays for resacking the grain and loading it onto the buyer's truck. Once the grain arrives in the regional wholesaler's market, there are several market outlets. The grain may be sold in

Figure 2.3 Market structure and flows, 1995/96

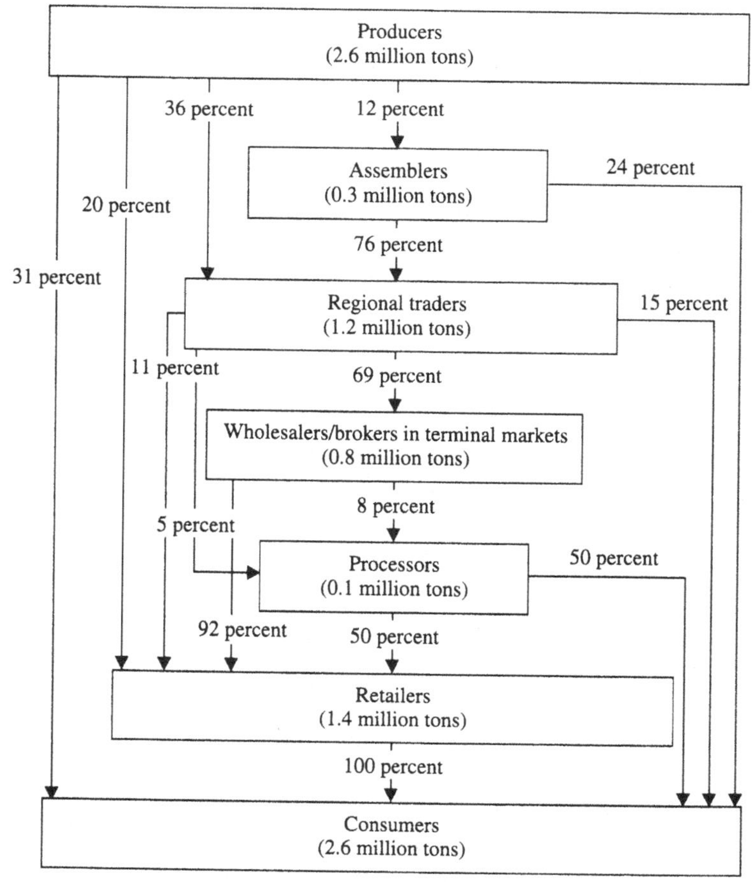

Source: Calculated from Gebremeskel, Jayne, and Shaffer 1998.

large quantities to local relief agencies, in smaller quantities to retailers or hotels, or in very small quantities directly to consumers.

Retailers

In the regional markets located in deficit areas or urban centers, retailers purchase grain in semiwholesale quantities (less than 1 ton) from the regional wholesalers. They can also purchase directly from farmers, from mills, or from the central market using the services of brokers.

Consumers

As noted earlier, since reform consumers have had a number of supply sources. They can purchase grain directly from farmers, from assemblers, from regional traders, from processors (mills), or from retailers.

The Relative Importance of Market Outlets

The marketing chain just described and the relative importance of the different market outlets is presented in Figure 2.3. At the farmgate level, the volume of direct sales to consumers is surprisingly high, 31 percent of total sales, while sales to rural assemblers play a minor role, comprising only 12 percent of sales. The most important pattern is seen in sales by farmers directly to regional traders, which make up 36 percent of producers' sales. The bulk of sales by rural assemblers (76 percent) are to the regional traders. Overall, regional traders handle 45 percent of the total domestic marketed surplus, or 1.2 million tons. In turn, most of the sales by the regional traders (nearly 70 percent) are made in the terminal markets, either through the services of brokers or directly to regional wholesalers, constituting of roughly 800,000 tons. Either regional traders or brokers in the terminal markets sell grain (mainly wheat) to processors, their sales constituting 40 percent of the total marketed quantity of wheat, or some 120,000 tons. Of the 54 percent of the total marketable surplus that is passed through retailers, the largest share is procured from wholesalers (740,000 tons), followed by that purchased directly from farmers (520,000 tons). Finally, as expected, consumers purchase a large share of their total grain from retailers, 55 percent or 1.43 million tons. However, a surprisingly large share of purchases, 31 percent, are made directly from producers. This confirms the relatively unsophisticated nature of the market and shows that most of the transformation of unprocessed grains is undertaken by consumers themselves. In particular, it is surprising that processors have not acquired a more significant role in the market in the wake of market reforms. Recent studies reveal that one of the dramatic effects of market reforms in eastern and southern Africa is the emergence of small-scale maize mills that have significantly reduced consumer prices (Jayne et al. 1999).

Issues Related to the Marketing Chain

When viewing the marketing chain from producer to consumer, several important points emerge. First, relatively little, if any, transformation of grain takes place along the marketing chain. With the exception of wheat, which can be sold in the form of flour, the bulk of Ethiopian grain is sold in an unprocessed form. For this reason, consumers may not care whether they buy grain from producers or from retailers, and may even prefer to buy from producers to reduce their costs. This suggests that, beyond transport and limited storage, relatively few market services are provided by intermediaries, indicating a relatively unsophisticated market structure.

Second, it is common practice for the sack in which the grain is transported to be changed at every transfer of ownership within the marketing chain. From the farmgate to the consumer, there can be up to five resackings. Each change of sack entails handling and sewing costs, in addition to the cost of the sack itself, ultimately raising total marketing costs and the price faced by the consumer. Traders consider resacking a necessity because it enables them to physically assess both the weight and the quality of the grain, as well as to ascertain the quality of the sack (to reduce transport and storage losses).

Third, the absence of a system of grades and standards for grain causes traders to trade either with regular partners whom they know well or with brokers with whom they work exclusively. This has the result of decreasing the size of the market and the frequency of transactions.

Summary

The dramatic market reform implemented by the Ethiopian government in 1990 has remained fairly coherent and internally driven. As anticipated, it had the significant effect of raising producer prices while reducing consumer prices, thus reducing the marketing margin between surplus and deficit areas. However, margins remain fairly high, and their volatility has not decreased as much as have their absolute levels. Another indication of market improvement since reform is the increase in short-term and long-term market integration.

Grain production in Ethiopia is characterized by the geographical dispersion of surplus zones and deficit zones, resulting in a natural incentive to trade. Production is highly rain-dependent and thus is marked by a seasonal pattern of both production and marketing in which postharvest sales occur mainly in January through March, resulting in depressed prices during this period. Despite the seasonal pattern, there is little evidence of forward contracting to reduce producer price risks.

A significant share of the Ethiopian population, 42 percent, is market-dependent, and 23 million people are considered food-deficit, with a food gap of 1.4 million tons. Like grain supply, the demand for grain is geographically dispersed, with a high concentration of demand in the nation's capital and central market, Addis Ababa.

Market infrastructure is severely constrained in Ethiopia. Transport infrastructure is limited mainly to roads, and the country has one of the world's lowest road densities. Nearly half of the rural population does not have access to all-weather roads. Although 72 percent of grain production is retained for on-farm uses, weak storage infrastructure results in large storage losses and vulnerability of the grain to moisture and pests. Some 2,200 modern warehouses were built during the monopoly era, with a total capacity of 1 million tons, but these facilities are largely inaccessible to the private sector, with less than 50 percent use.

The structure of the market has increased in complexity since market reform was implemented. However, there remains significant scope for increasing the scale and the sophistication of the market. Of the total grain production in 1995/96, only 28 percent or 2.6 million tons was marketed. Of the marketed quantity, nearly one-third was sold by producers directly to consumers. The remaining 68 percent of the marketed surplus was distributed to regional traders (36 percent), retailers (20 percent), and assemblers (12 percent). Regional traders handled 46 percent of the total volume marketed, while brokers in the central market handled 31 percent. An analysis of the marketing chain suggests that there is still significant room for increasing the market roles of both traders and brokers. Also, processors play a very limited role, indicating that very little value is added to the marketed goods, beyond transfer across space, throughout the marketing chain. Another issue is the high cost of handling the grain due to the need for visual inspection of both quantities and qualities, in the absence of a system of grades and standards. The following chapter addresses these themes through an analysis of primary data on individual traders' asset portfolios and arbitrage behavior.

CHAPTER 3

Traders' Market Behavior

Survey and Data

The data used in this study are drawn from a survey of wholesale traders in 12 markets that was conducted in two rounds between May and December 1996. The criteria for the selection of study regions were the representativeness of regions in terms of type of grain, net market position (surplus versus deficit), geographical distribution, and importance to the national market. Surplus areas are defined as areas with a significant marketable surplus for export to other regions of the country. The survey included three surplus areas, each representing a different traded grain: Western Wellega zone in Oromiya region, which is a maize surplus area; Arsi zone in central Oromiya region, which is a surplus area for wheat and barley; and Western Gojam zone in Amhara region, which is a teff surplus area. Conversely, deficit areas are defined as areas that have a net grain deficit and import grain from other areas of the country. The survey included three deficit areas: South Wello zone in Amhara region, Tigray region, and the Harar/Dire Dawa region in eastern Ethiopia. It also included Addis Ababa, representing the central market, as a seventh study region.

Markets within each region were selected on the basis of their importance as centers of wholesale grain trade and as transit points for grain flows across the country. The markets surveyed were Nekempte and Jaji in Western Wellega, Assela and Sagure in Arsi, Bahir Dar and Bure in Western Gojam, Dessie and Kombolcha in South Wello, and Mekele in Tigray, as well as Dire Dawa, Harar, and Addis Ababa. The principal grains included in the study were teff, wheat, and maize.

A sample of wholesale traders was obtained by first undertaking a census of traders engaged in wholesale activities who were present in the market on the day of the survey visit (a market day). Sample respondents were randomly selected from the total trader population present. Given the unavailability of a census of traders from official sources, this method was considered the least biased alternative. The total sample included 152 wholesale traders representing 6 percent of the estimated population of wholesalers in the country.

In order to obtain a panel data set, the same traders in each market were interviewed twice, with an interval of four months. The first round of interviews was conducted just prior to the rainy season, in May and June, when trading slows down. In contrast, the second round of interviews was carried out during the harvest season in October and November, when traders are very busy buying grain from farmers. Despite the intensification of activities in the second round and the change of occupation of some traders, the attrition rate of traders was relatively low, with only 16 percent of the initial sample dropping out of the second round of interviews.

The trader survey instrument was designed to obtain a complete picture of each trader's grain business activities: contractual choices, agency relations with brokers, volume and direction of flows, transaction costs related to market search, physical resources and assets, demographic characteristics, working capital and access to credit, and social capital. In the first round of interviews, traders responded to questions that caused them to recall their activities for the past six months, from the beginning of the harvest year in December 1995. In the second round the traders recalled their activities for the four months since the last interview.

The survey focused on two types of transaction costs related to search: the costs of search labor and the costs of holding capital fixed in grain inventory during the search process. With respect to search labor, information was collected on the number of minutes spent daily gathering market information, the number of traders consulted daily, the number of person-days required to conduct a transaction, the number of offers considered prior to completing a transaction, and the number of employees engaged in searches. In addition, information was obtained on traders' access to additional labor, such as the number of family members able to step in if necessary, and the traders' other occupations.

With respect to the cost of capital, the survey collected information on the amount of working capital held by traders, the frequency of turnover of capital, minimum levels of working capital available during the year, and the sources (banks, friends, family, suppliers, savings associations) and amounts of credit they obtained. In addition, information was obtained on traders' access to additional capital, such as how many creditors they had available, whether they had parents in the grain business, whether they owned collateral assets such as a house or vehicle, and whether they had inherited their businesses.

Data on social capital, or the extent of traders' "connectedness," were obtained through questions regarding the number of local and distant market contacts, the number of distant markets in which traders had contacts, the number of contacts from the same region, the number of family members and friends in grain trade, the number of regular partners traders had in local and distant markets, and the number of languages traders spoke.

Traders were asked about their use of different contractual arrangements in several ways. First, traders were asked in general terms whether they used intermediaries regularly and to state their rationale for working with a broker, as well as detailed questions on their agency relations. They were also asked to recall what proportion of their total transactions occurred in local markets and in distant markets. They were then asked to detail the proportion of their local and distant transactions that they conducted with intermediaries, including both agents and brokers. This provided detailed data, collected in two rounds, on the traders' relative use of six contractual options: local agents, distant agents, local brokers, distant brokers, local self-search, and distant self-search. This information was gathered for purchases and sales separately. Finally, traders responded to a third set of questions related to their contractual choices. They were asked to describe their last transaction, specifically whether they used a broker, how much the commission fee was, how much time it took the broker to search, and how transparent the broker's operations were.

Trader Characteristics

The survey results (Table 3.1) reveal that traders at the wholesaler level are overwhelmingly male; 94 percent of the sample were male. Two-thirds of the sample were Christian Orthodox, and nearly 70 percent of the sample spoke the national language, Amharic, as their mother tongue, followed

Table 3.1 Demographic characteristics of traders, 1996

		Gender		Religion		Mother tongue		Father's occupation		Mother's occupation	
Type of market		Male	Female	Muslim	Orthodox	Amharic	Oromigna	Grain trade	Farmer	Grain trade	Housewife
Surplus											
Nekempte	*N*	8	1	6	2	2	7	4	2	0	6
	Percent	89	11	67	22	22	78	57	29	0	86
Jaji	*N*	3	1	4	0	2	2	1	3	1	30
	Percent	75	25	100	0	50	50	25	75	25	75
Assela	*N*	7	0	3	4	1	6	3	4	0	7
	Percent	100	0	43	57	14	86	43	57	0	100
Sagure	*N*	5	0	1	4	1	4	0	4	0	4
	Percent	100	0	20	80	20	80	0	100	0	100
Bahir Dar	*N*	29	1	3	27	29	1	11	6	0	18
	Percent	97	3	10	90	97	3	50	27	0	82
Bure	*N*	9	0	1	8	9	0	3	4	0	60
	Percent	100	0	11	89	100	0	38	50	0	75
Subtotal	*N*	61	3	18	45	44	20	22	23	1	44
	Percent	95	5	28	70	69	31	42	44	2	85
Deficit											
Dessie	*N*	14	0	13	1	14	0	6	2	0	11
	Percent	100	0	93	7	100	0	50	17	0	92
Kombolcha	*N*	5	0	3	2	5	0	2	3	0	3
	Percent	100	0	60	40	100	0	40	60	0	60
Mekele	*N*	14	0	2	12	1	0	2	7	1	8
	Percent	100	0	14	86	7	0	17	58	8	67
Dire Dawa	*N*	7	2	0	9	9	0	4	2	1	4
	Percent	78	22	0	100	100	0	50	25	13	50
Harar	*N*	6	3	0	9	8	1	6	3	2	6
	Percent	67	33	0	100	89	11	67	33	22	67
Subtotal	*N*	46	5	18	33	37	1	20	17	4	32
	Percent	90	10	35	65	73	2	43	37	9	70
Central											
Addis Ababa	*N*	36	1	13	23	24	6	20	10	2	26
	Percent	97	3	35	62	65	16	67	33	7	87
Total	Percent	94	6	32	66	69	18	48	39	5	80

Source: Author's survey, 1996.

by Oromigna (18 percent), Tigrigna (9 percent), and Gurage (5 percent). Traders appear to carry on the trading activities of their fathers; nearly half of traders indicated that their fathers were occupied in grain trade. This finding implies that a significant amount of social capital may be derived from carrying on the family grain trade business. Mothers' occupation in grain trade did not appear to be significant.

Generally, traders did not appear to switch businesses very often; the total number of years the traders surveyed had worked in grain trading was only slightly higher than the number of years they had been in their current businesses, 10 and 8 years, respectively (Table 3.2). At the time of the survey in 1996, traders indicated that they had worked in their current businesses since before the reform in 1990. This suggests that trading businesses had operated from within the parallel economy even prior to reform. Finally, there appears to have been relatively little variation within the sample in terms of years of schooling or age; traders had received 10 years of schooling on average, and the average age of those in the sample was 33.

Table 3.2 Human capital of traders, 1996

Type of market (*N*)		Years in trade	Years operating this business	Years of education	Age
Surplus					
Nekempte	Mean (SD)	5 (6)	3 (2)	11 (2)	24 (4)
(*N*)		9	9	9	9
Jaji	Mean (SD)	17 (7)	15 (9)	10 (2)	20 (1)
(*N*)		4	4	4	4
Assela	Mean (SD)	17 (12)	11 (7)	9 (3)	44 (8)
(*N*)		7	7	7	7
Sagure	Mean (SD)	20 (15)	6 (4)	5 (2)	54 (12)
(*N*)		5	5	5	5
Bahir Dar	Mean (SD)	8 (7)	5 (4)	11 (3)	30 (12)
(*N*)		30	30	30	30
Bure	Mean (SD)	8 (6)	5 (4)	8 (3)	32 (10)
(*N*)		9	9	9	9
Subtotal	Mean (SD)	10 (9)	6 (5)	10 (3)	32 (13)
(*N*)		64	64	64	64
Deficit					
Dessie	Mean (SD)	17 (12)	13 (12)	8 (5)	41 (18)
(*N*)		14	14	14	14
Kombolcha	Mean (SD)	6 (3)	5 (3)	10 (4)	28 (5)
(*N*)		5	5	5	5
Mekele	Mean (SD)	10 (9)	7 (7)	7 (3)	36 (9)
(*N*)		14	14	13	14
Dire Dawa	Mean (SD)	11 (9)	11 (9)	11 (3)	30 (7)
(*N*)		9	9	9	9
Harar	Mean (SD)	9 (4)	8 (4)	9 (5)	31 (15)
(*N*)		9	9	9	9
Subtotal	Mean (SD)	11 (9)	9 (9)	9 (4)	34 (13)
(*N*)		51	51	50	51
Central					
Addis Ababa	Mean (SD)	10 (7)	9 (7)	11 (3)	32 (10)
(*N*)		37	37	37	37
Total	Mean (SD)	10 (9)	8 (7)	10 (4)	33 (12)
(*N*)		152	152	151	152

Source: Author's survey, 1996.

Firms and Their Resources

Status and Ownership of Firms

As elsewhere in sub-Saharan Africa, grain businesses in Ethiopia are small operations, started and managed by their owners and operating with relatively few fixed investments. Although the trading businesses sampled were identified as wholesale firms, 25 percent of the sample identified themselves as mainly retailers with some wholesale activity, while 3 percent of the sample identified themselves as assemblers, suggesting a lack of specialization (Table 3.3). Eighty percent of current owners had started up their trading businesses rather than inheriting or buying them. This suggests that a trading firm does not acquire a business identity or reputation outside of the identity of the owner, implying that grain-trading businesses are likely to be small and personalized. The close identification of a business with the current owner was further confirmed in that, for the majority of businesses, the owner was also the manager of the day-to-day operations. Thus, in both surplus and deficit regions roughly three-quarters of firms had owners who also managed them. In the central market the proportion is lower; 54 percent of firms have owner-managers. Finally, the extent of specialization of grain-trading businesses varies considerably

Table 3.3 Business characteristics of traders, 1996

Type of market		Business classification: Assembly	Wholesale	Retail	Percent owner start-up	Percent sole owner	Percent owner-manager	Percent owner with other business
Surplus								
Nekempte	*N*	0	6	3	9	9	4	3
	Percent	0	67	33	100	100	44	33
Jaji	*N*	0	3	1	4	4	0	3
	Percent	0	75	25	100	100	0	75
Assela	*N*	0	7	0	6	7	7	1
	Percent	0	100	0	86	100	100	14
Sagure	*N*	1	4	0	5	4	4	2
	Percent	20	80	0	100	80	80	40
Bahir Dar	*N*	1	23	6	23	28	24	16
	Percent	3	77	20	77	93	80	53
Bure	*N*	0	7	2	5	9	8	7
	Percent	0	78	22	56	100	89	78
Subtotal	*N*	2	50	12	52	61	47	32
	Percent	3	78	19	81	95	73	50
Deficit								
Dessie	*N*	1	7	6	14	14	10	3
	Percent	7	50	43	100	100	71	21
Kombolcha	*N*	0	3	2	4	5	5	1
	Percent	0	60	40	80	100	100	20
Mekele	*N*	0	11	3	13	12	14	5
	Percent	0	79	21	93	86	100	36
Dire Dawa	*N*	0	3	6	7	9	2	2
	Percent	0	33	67	78	100	22	22
Harar	*N*	0	6	3	9	9	8	4
	Percent	0	67	33	100	100	89	44
Subtotal	*N*	1	30	20	47	49	39	15
	Percent	2	59	39	92	96	76	29
Central								
Addis Ababa	*N*	2	29	6	23	32	20	4
	Percent	5	78	16		86	54	11
Total	Percent	3	72	25	80	93	70	34

Source: Author's survey, 1996.

between markets. Overall, only one-third of firms are engaged in other business activities outside of grain trade. However, the range for different markets varies from 14 percent to 78 percent of firms.

Firm Assets

Few trading firms invest in transport vehicles; only 6 percent of the traders sampled owned vehicles. In contrast, traders in small markets such as Jaji and Sagure own their warehouses, compared to the majority of traders (70 percent), who rent storage space, often from the government (Table 3.4). A relatively high proportion of traders (39 percent) own telephones, and generally all traders appear to have access to telephones. At the same time, traders place relatively few telephone orders for their businesses. This is an important finding, suggesting that the lack of use of telecommunications in grain trading is not due to infrastructural constraints as much as to other factors. Finally, a significant share of traders, roughly half, has electricity. Surprisingly, traders outside of the central market have much better access to electricity than do those in Addis Ababa.

The average storage capacity of traders within markets varies considerably, indicating the different storage behavior in the different markets (Table 3.5). Thus, traders in the Wellega zone had relatively little storage

Table 3.4 Business assets of traders, 1996

Type of market		Percent own vehicle	Percent own warehouse	Percent rent storage	Percent own telephone	Percent have access to telephone	Percent have electricity
Surplus							
Nekempte	*N*	0	1	9	3	6	9
	Percent	0	11	100	33	100	100
Jaji	*N*	2	4	0	3	1	4
	Percent	50	100	0	75	100	100
Assela	*N*	0	2	6	2	5	5
	Percent	0	29	86	29	100	71
Sagure	*N*	2	5	0	2	3	3
	Percent	40	100	0	40	100	60
Bahir Dar	*N*	1	11	21	6	23	8
	Percent	3	38	81	20	100	27
Bure	*N*	0	7	4	1	8	7
	Percent	0	78	50	11	100	78
Subtotal	*N*	5	30	40	17	46	36
	Percent	8	48	70	27	100	56
Deficit							
Dessie	*N*	1	5	8	9	4	13
	Percent	7	36	62	64	100	93
Kombolcha	*N*						
	Percent		60	40		100	100
Mekele	*N*	1	7	7	6	5	6
	Percent	7	50	50	43	83	43
Dire Dawa	*N*		6	4	6	3	5
	Percent		67	44	67	100	56
Harar	*N*		6	2	6	3	8
	Percent		67	22	67	100	89
Subtotal	*N*	2	27	23	27	20	37
	Percent	4	53	46	53	95	73
Central							
Addis Ababa	*N*	2	4	36	15	22	5
	Percent	5	11	97	41	100	14
Total	Percent	6	40	69	39	99	51

Source: Author's survey, 1996.

capacity (383 to 519 quintals) compared to the average of 1,156 quintals for the sample (1 quintal is equivalent to 100 kilograms). The average number of days grain was stored during the marketing year, 16 to 21 days, was also lower for this area compared to more than twice that for the sample. This might be explained by the fact that maize is more subject to storage losses due to its greater moisture content. In contrast, traders in the Arsi zone, who trade mainly barley and wheat, had the greatest storage capacity and the largest number of storage days. Strikingly, traders in Assela stored grain for 92 days, roughly twice the sample average, over the year. According to field interviews, this was not a usual practice, but rather a response to falling wheat prices due to the unfavorable timing of food aid shipments of wheat. Overall, neither the storage capacity nor the days stored on average varied significantly by type of market, with traders in surplus, deficit, and central markets storing grain for about 50 days on average over the year.

Although only one-third of the traders sampled received formal bank loans, all received credit over the marketing year. The survey reveals that traders have access to substantial levels of credit; those sampled received on average Eth. Birr 89,000 over the year, which corresponds to US$14,000

Table 3.5 Firm resources: Physical, human, and financial, 1996

Type of market		Total storage capacity (100-kg bags)	Days storage	Total employees	Total credit (Eth. Birr)[a]	Working capital (Eth. Birr)
Surplus						
Nekempte	Mean (SD)	383 (177)	16 (9)	7 (1)	23,778 (35,138)	27,500 (31,168)
(*N*)		9	9	9	9	8
Jaji	Mean (SD)	519 (344)	21 (13)	11 (6)	100,750 (97,233)	53,333 (41,633))
(*N*)		4	4	4	4	3
Assela	Mean (SD)	2,486 (1,633)	92 (72)	8 (2)	75,786 (55,963)	45,000 (34,278)
(*N*)		7	7	7	7	7
Sagure	Mean (SD)	3,875 (4,131)	43 (38)	8 (7)	23,0400 (19,2683)	37,750 (44,724)
(*N*)		4	5	4	5	4
Bahir Dar	Mean (SD)	653 (491)	49 (32)	8 (4)	78,807 (116,065)	62,367 (53,811)
(*N*)		30	30	30	30	30
Bure	Mean (SD)	1,083 (1,440)	50 (24)	9 (8)	79,444 (102,372)	30,375 (25,054)
(*N*)		9	9	9	9	8
Subtotal	Mean (SD)	1,076 (1,543)	47 (39)	8 (4)	84,043 (114,257)	49,333 (45,878)
(*N*)		63	64	63	64	60
Deficit						
Dessie	Mean (SD)	1,773 (2,588)	28 (19)	7 (4)	29,564 (48,531)	104,375 (122,982)
(*N*)		14	14	14	14	8
Kombolcha	Mean (SD)	1,810 (3,186)	43 (40)	6 (1)	42,700 (46,424)	29,000 (19,494)
(*N*)		5	5	5	5	5
Mekele	Mean (SD)	750 (971)	63 (45)	6 (4)	99,000 (220,831)	56,000 (56,804)
(*N*)		14	14	14	14	10
Dire Dawa	Mean (SD)	506 (339)	47 (32)	4 (3)	27,784 (22,384)	30,000 (14,577)
(*N*)		8	9	9	9	9
Harar	Mean (SD)	1,767 (1,818)	37 (36)	5 (3)	91,111 (115,941)	102,222 (92,976)
(*N*)		9	9	9	9	9
Subtotal	Mean (SD)	1,287 (1,932)	44 (36)	6 (3)	60,460 (129,503)	66,585 (79,116)
(*N*)		50	51	51	51	41
Central						
Addis Ababa	Mean (SD)	1,114 (1,703)	47 (49)	8 (6)	136,573 (388,609)	51,172 (66,512)
(*N*)		37	37	36	37	29
Total	Mean (SD)	1,156 (1,711)	46 (41)	7 (5)	88,917 (218,733)	55,185 (62,647)
(*N*)		150	152	150	152	130

Source: Author's survey, 1996.

[a] Eth. Birr 6.35 = US$1 in 1995/96.

(Table 3.5). This is a significantly greater amount than the average per capita income (US$110) for the country. Similarly, the traders sampled had fairly large amounts of working capital (Table 3.5), ranging from US$7,700 to US$10,000, which is a significantly larger amount than recent survey results (Gabre-Madhin et al. 2001) indicate for Benin (US$1,470) and Malawi (US$560). In all markets, traders have greater amounts of total credit than working capital. Working capital is defined as the amount of money that traders regularly have at their disposal for the purposes of buying and selling grain, while total credit refers to the sum of all the loans they receive over the course of a year for their trading business. These are different in that credit is cumulative and can be used for purposes other than buying and selling grain; for instance, it can be applied to the fixed costs of the business.

Traders in the central market of Addis Ababa appear to have significantly more access to credit than do those in other markets. It remains somewhat of a puzzle why, although the average amount of credit for Addis Ababa traders is one and a half times greater than the sample average, the amount of working capital of traders in Addis Ababa falls below the sample average. There appears

Figure 3.1 Grain flows and distances between study markets, 1995/96

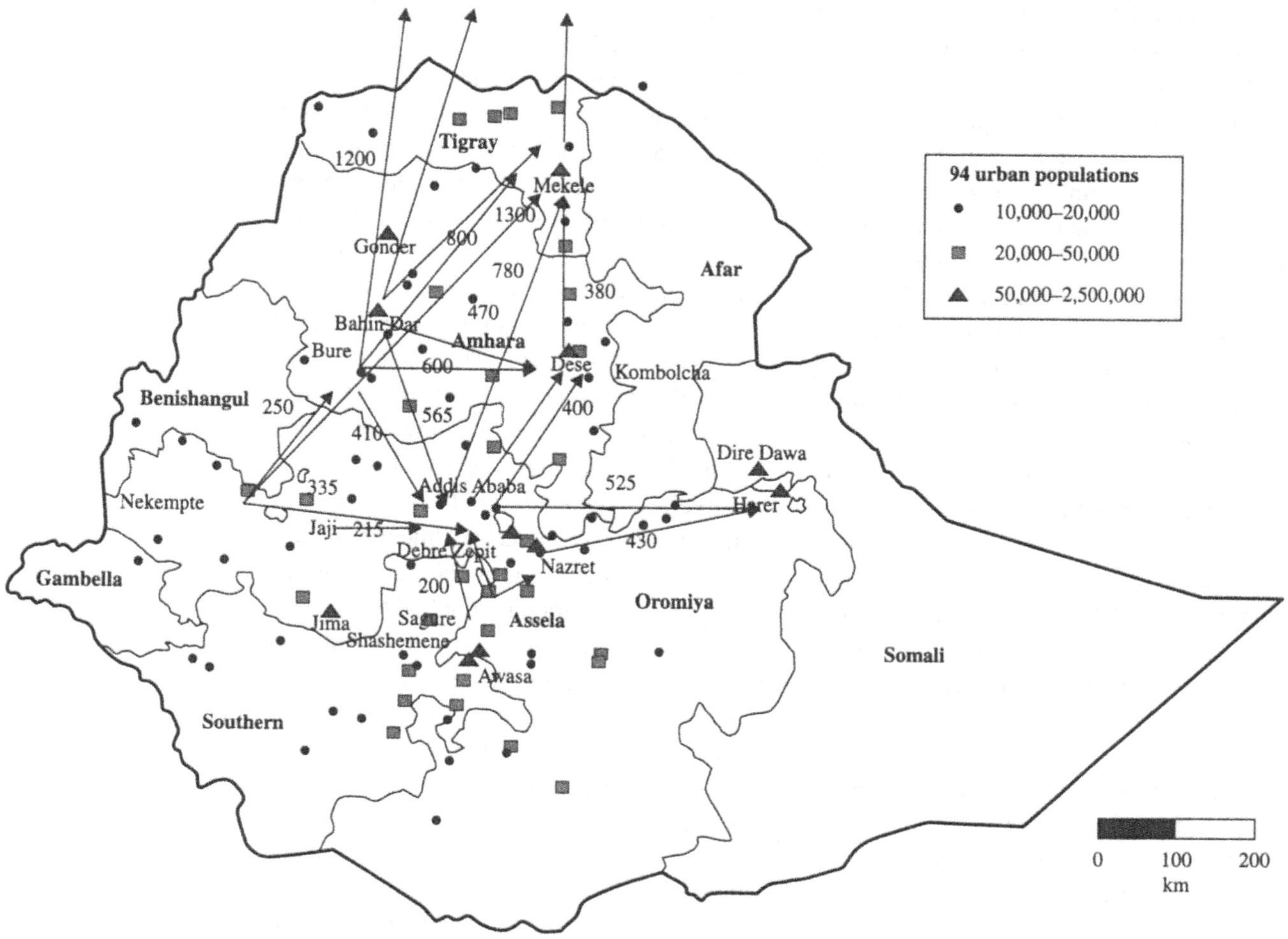

Source: United Nations Development Program 1998 (http://www.undp.org).
Note: Distances in kilometers. All borders are approximate and unofficial.

to be little variation in markets in terms of human resources. Generally, trading firms are small enterprises composed of seven to eight employees, including the owner.

The Spatial Pattern of Grain Flows

Survey evidence for the study markets confirms the radial configuration of grain flows, with the Addis Ababa market operating as a national hub for grain flows. Market flows cover considerable distances, ranging from 200 to 1,200 kilometers. As shown in Figure 3.1, although flows in and out of Addis Ababa dominate the pattern of flows, new market channels are emerging because of new roads that link rural areas. Thus, there is also evidence of flows directly from producer regions in Wellega and Gojam zones to deficit areas of Tigray and Wello.

In the major maize-producing zones of western Oromiya, the main supply areas for the Nekempte and Jaji markets are nearby producer markets as well as the markets themselves, where traders buy directly from producers. The main destination for grain purchased in these markets is Addis Ababa, located at a distance of 330 kilometers from Nekempte and 215 kilometers from Jaji. In addition to this main channel, some respondents reported that there are secondary flows to Bure in the Gojam zone of Amhara region, located 270 kilometers away. One respondent also indicated that he had made one direct sale in Mekele in Tigray region, at a distance of 1,300 kilometers. However, the respondent noted that this sale was too difficult and costly to repeat.

In the wheat- and barley-producing zones of Arsi, the Assela and Sagure markets are supplied by surrounding producer markets and their own markets. The principal destination of grain from these markets is Addis Ababa, located 175 and 200 kilometers away, respectively. Other destinations include Nazareth and Debre Zeit, located 75 and 125 kilometers away, respectively, on the Addis Ababa route. Nazareth appears to function as a secondary hub through which grain from Arsi and other nearby areas flows to the terminal markets of Harar and Dire Dawa (425 kilometers away). In addition to trading directly in the Addis Ababa market, traders also reported that they delivered wheat directly to wheat mills in Akaki, on the outskirts of Addis Ababa, and barley to the brewery in Assela.

In the major teff-producing zone of Western Gojam, the survey revealed a dynamic transformation of marketing channels in the Bure and Bahir Dar markets, with multiple-destination markets and an evolution away from the traditional dominance of the Addis Ababa market axis. As in the other surplus regions, these markets were supplied mainly by nearby markets and by producers in the markets themselves. In contrast to the other surplus markets, however, the survey revealed numerous-destination markets. Thus, flows from Bahir Dar to Addis Ababa were surpassed by flows directly to Mekele (744 kilometers), Adigrat, and other markets in Tigray; to Dessie (470 kilometers) and Kombolcha in Wello zone; and to Gonder in Amhara region, in addition to Asmara, the capital city of neighboring Eritrea (1,000 kilometers distant). Similarly, important channels have emerged from Bure to Mekele (600 kilometers) and Asmara, Eritrea (1,200 kilometers), although the channel to Addis Ababa (410 kilometers) remains primary.

Thus, among the study markets, grain flows into Addis Ababa were observed from Nekempte, Jaji, Assela, Sagure, Bure, and Bahir Dar. Grain flows out of Addis Ababa were observed to Harar and Dire Dawa, in the eastern part of the country, located 525 kilometers away and served by rail transport in the case of Dire Dawa. A second major destination of grain flowing out of Addis Ababa was the Wello zone of Amhara region, specifically Dessie and Kombolcha, at a distance of 400 kilometers. Grain flows were also observed from Addis Ababa to the Mekele market, located 780 kilometers away, as well as to Asmara in neighboring Eritrea.

In addition to receiving flows from Bure, Bahir Dar, and Addis Ababa, the Mekele market was supplied from Dessie, as well as nearby producer markets. Although Mekele can be considered a terminal market in that the majority of grain is supplied to the local population, there were also flows outward from Mekele, to Adigrat in Tigray region as well as to Asmara in Eritrea. In contrast to Dessie, which relied heavily on supplies from distant markets such as Addis Ababa, Bure, and Bahir Dara, the Kombolcha market was supplied by nearby producer markets in addition to these distant markets. In addition to receiving flows from Addis Ababa, the Harar and Dire Dawa markets were supplied by Debre Zeit and Nazareth, also on the railway line. Harar was supplied by nearby producer markets. Both Harar and Dire Dawa functioned as terminal markets, with little outward flow.

Marketing Margins and Profits

Traders surveyed provided detailed evidence regarding their most recently completed wholesale transaction, defined as a transaction in which a given quantity of grain was purchased and sold. Information was also collected on the various attributes of this transaction: the total kilometric distance involved from purchase to sale, the number of suppliers from whom they purchased grain and the number of clients to whom they sold it, and the quantity transacted. In addition, detailed information was obtained on all the marketing costs incurred from purchase to

Table 3.6 Attributes of last transaction by type of market, 1996

Type of market		Total distance traded (km)	Number of suppliers	Number of clients	Ratio supplier/ client	Quantity purchased (quintals)[a]
Surplus						
Nekempte	Mean (SD)	331 (0)	5 (7)	1 (0)	5 (7)	222 (258)
	N	3	7	7	7	16
Jaji	Mean (SD)	215 (0)	73 (57)	1 (0)	73 (57)	68 (30)
	N	4	4	4	4	8
Assela	Mean (SD)	202 (31)	16 (18)	1 (1)	16 (7)	83 (73)
	N	7	7	7	7	14
Sagure	Mean (SD)	203 (7)	93 (78)	26 (50)	68 (90)	110 (110)
	N	4	4	4	4	9
Bahir Dar	Mean (SD)	177 (206)	4 (10)	8 (21)	3 (11)	147 (180)
	N	20	22	22	22	52
Bure	Mean (SD)	331 (358)	52 (51)	1 (0)	52 (51)	116 (50)
	N	8	7	8	7	17
Subtotal	Mean (SD)	223 (205)	25 (43)	6 (19)	22 (42)	137 (164)
	N	46	51	52	51	116
Deficit						
Dessie	Mean (SD)	369 (103)	2 (2)	74 (32)	0 (0)	171 (134)
	N	11	10	10	9	26
Kombolcha	Mean (SD)	243 (180)	1 (1)	28 (19)	0 (0)	90 (112)
	N	5	5	3	3	10
Mekele	Mean (SD)	181 (290)	1 (1)	29 (31)	1 (1)	91 (54)
	N	12	12	12	12	26
Dire Dawa	Mean (SD)	139 (215)	1 (1)	108 (115)	0 (0)	97 (105)
	N	6	6	6	6	15
Harar	Mean (SD)	323 (226)	2 (1)	110 (101)	0 (0)	213 (309)
	N	9	9	9	9	18
Subtotal	Mean (SD)	260 (225)	2 (1)	70 (75)	0 (1)	137 (168)
	N	43	42	40	39	95
Central						
Addis Ababa	Mean (SD)	34 (107)	2 (2)	3 (5)	2 (2)	472 (2,223)
	N	30	30	30	30	67
Total	Mean (SD)	189 (213)	11 (30)	26 (54)	10 (29)	218 (1,104)
	N	119	123	122	120	278

Source: Author's survey, 1996.

[a] A quintal is equivalent to 100 kilograms.

sale as well as the purchase and sale prices. These data enabled the calculation of the gross marketing margin (defined as the difference between purchase and sale price), the total marketing costs, and the net margin or profit (defined as the residual after marketing costs are deducted from the gross margin). Clearly the net margin includes returns that may be attributed factors of marketing whose costs are not explicitly included in the set of marketing costs, such as managerial inputs, as well as partner search, enforcement, and information gathering.

As shown in Table 3.6, traders in both surplus and deficit markets appear to trade grain over similar distances (223 to 260 kilometers on average), while traders in the central market have much smaller distances (34 on average) to travel, as expected. The number of suppliers and clients involved in a transaction provides an indication of the structure of the marketing chain. Thus, in rural markets in surplus areas, traders tend to buy from a large number of suppliers, such as farmers as well as collection agents. As markets get larger, traders buy in larger quantities from a small number of suppliers, and these are more likely to be other traders rather than farmers. In deficit areas the converse is true, in that traders are likely to buy grain in large quantities from wholesalers in distant markets and to sell the grain in small quantities to retailers as well as directly to consumers. The survey results reveal that traders in smaller rural markets in surplus zones, such as Jaji, Sagure, and Bure purchase from a large number of suppliers (farmers), while traders in larger wholesale markets in the surplus zones purchase from a relatively small number of suppliers, mostly collection agents. In general, the number of clients is considerably smaller than the number of suppliers for traders in the surplus zones, indicating that traders buy in numerous small transactions and bulk up for sale to a single wholesaler in their destination market. Thus, the ratio of suppliers to clients for the surplus zones is 22 on average.

As expected, the evidence suggests that in the deficit markets traders purchase large quantities from a small number of agents (Table 3.6), typically wholesalers located in the central market. They then sell the grain purchased to many clients, suggesting that they both sell to retailers and sell in retail quantities themselves. Thus, the ratio of suppliers to clients is very low, between 0 and 1. Finally, traders in the central market appear to be engaged mainly in wholesale trade for both purchase and sale, with relatively few suppliers and relatively few clients. Thus, the ratio of suppliers to clients for the Addis Ababa market is 2. These results suggest that traders in the regional markets are not specialized in wholesale activities, but rather are engaged in assembly and bulking-up activities in the surplus areas and in retail distribution in the deficit areas.

In terms of the quantities transacted, traders in surplus and deficit areas have surprisingly similar capacities, with 137 quintals (1.4 tons) exchanged per transaction, varying from 68 to 222 quintals (Table 3.6). Traders in Addis Ababa, however, engage in transactions involving significantly larger, highly variable quantities, on average 472 quintals. These results suggest that there is a locational advantage to trade in the central market, with traders tending to have better access to credit and to be more specialized in wholesale activities.

Absolute Margins and Costs

In absolute terms, gross marketing margins appear to be 2 and 3 times higher in the regional markets than in the central market (Table 3.7). This is because traders in the Addis Ababa market both buy and sell locally, as noted earlier. On average, marketing margins in surplus and deficit areas are Eth. Birr 28 and 21 per quintal. However, there is a surprising amount of variation between markets in the surplus areas. In particular, Bure, which is located in the Gojam zone, has an especially high average marketing margin of Eth. Birr 51 per quintal.

Absolute marketing costs appear to follow a pattern similar to that of margins, with costs roughly similar in the surplus and deficit zones, in contrast to markedly lower costs in the Addis Ababa market (Table 3.7). Bure again shows an exceptional pattern, with significantly higher costs than elsewhere. In the deficit markets, traders in Harar and Dire Dawa appear to incur relatively low costs, which is puzzling given that distances of trade are not particularly small. Viewed as a percentage of the gross margin, relative costs vary from as low as 35 percent and 38 percent in Dire Dawa and Harar to 134 percent in Dessie and 124 percent in Jaji and Sagure, where traders appear to be trading at a loss. On average, marketing costs represent 83 percent of the gross margin.

Finally, traders' profits, calculated as the residual after deducting marketing costs from the gross margin, are roughly similar in absolute terms between surplus and deficit markets, Eth. Birr 5 and 4 per quintal, respectively (Table 3.7). At the same time, absolute profits vary considerably between markets. Thus, in surplus markets profits are relatively large in Bahir Dar and Bure, located in Gojam zone, compared to the very small

Table 3.7 Absolute marketing margins and costs by type of market, 1996

	Gross margin (Eth. Birr/quintal)[a]			Marketing costs (Eth. Birr/quintal)			Profit (Eth. Birr/quintal)			Costs as a percentage of gross margin		
Type of market	Mean	SD	*N*	Mean	SD	*N*	Mean	SD	*N*	Mean	SD	*N*
Surplus												
Nekempte	29	9	14	27	7	15	2	8	14	97	26	14
Jaji	17	6	8	20	6	8	−3	5	8	124	46	8
Assela	23	5	13	18	2	12	4	4	11	86	21	11
Sagure	15	3	8	17	4	6	−3	4	6	124	32	6
Bahir Dar	27	23	49	24	21	36	8	11	36	72	41	36
Bure	51	26	15	43	24	11	12	18	11	82	27	11
Subtotal	28	21	107	25	18	86	5	11	86	87	39	86
Deficit												
Dessie	18	6	25	26	26	15	−6	26	15	134	129	15
Kombolcha	17	4	10	12	7	5	6	5	5	64	30	5
Mekele	30	22	23	31	25	18	6	10	17	70	32	17
Dire Dawa	17	9	15	6	9	9	12	9	9	35	25	9
Harar	21	16	18	14	18	9	11	8	9	38	31	9
Subtotal	21	15	91	22	23	56	4	17	55	76	80	55
Central												
Addis Ababa	9	7	65	7	11	39	1	10	37	83	85	38
Total	22	21	264	21	20	187	5	15	179	83	65	180

Source: Author's survey, 1996.

[a] A quintal is equivalent to 100 kilograms. Eth. Birr 6.35 = US$1 in 1996.

or negative profits in the small rural markets of Jaji and Sagure. An explanation of the larger profits in Gojam is that traders are exploring new marketing channels, thus bypassing the Addis Ababa route in favor of direct trade routes to Mekele, Dessie, and Asmara.

In the case of the deficit markets there is a similarly wide range, with negative profits in Dessie and relatively high profits in Dire Dawa and Harar (Table 3.7). It is puzzling why profits in Dessie are negative while profits in nearby Kombolcha are positive. Traders' profits in the central market (Eth. Birr 1 per quintal) are significantly below the sample average of Eth. Birr 5, suggesting that traders in the central market are more specialized, operate on a larger scale, and are more competitive.

Costs and Profits Relative to Sales Revenue

So that the reader can compare the profitability of trading enterprises across the sample, Table 3.8 shows a breakdown of trade revenue for grain (equal to sale price) into the costs of acquiring the grain (purchase price), the costs of marketing the grain (marketing costs), and the remaining profit. Viewing these three elements relative to the sale price, one can see that, for the sample as a whole, the purchase price represents 82 percent of the sale price, marketing costs represent 16 percent of the sale price, and profits represent 2 percent of the sale price. Notwithstanding the considerable variation between markets, the high proportion of the sale price that is attributed to the purchase costs indicates that traders add relatively little value, in terms of transport, storage, or transformation of the grains in question. That is, the traders surveyed essentially undertake only spatial arbitrage in the case of the regional markets, and they are not engaged in either temporal arbitrage or arbitrage over form. In the case of surplus markets, where the bulk of locally produced grain is sold to distant markets, transport costs play a more important role, so the share of the sales revenue that is attributed to purchase price is

Table 3.8 Marketing costs and net profits relative to sale price by market, 1996

	Purchase price as a percentage of sale price		Marketing costs as a percentage of sale price		Net profit as a percentage of sale price		
Type of market	Mean	SD	Mean	SD	Mean	SD	*N*
Surplus							
Nekempte	63	8	36	13	1	10	14
Jaji	75	7	28	4	–4	8	8
Assela	83	3	14	3	3	3	11
Sagure	89	3	14	4	–2	3	6
Bahir Dar	75	16	19	15	6	9	36
Bure	65	18	24	11	7	10	11
Subtotal	74	15	22	14	3	12	86
Deficit							
Dessie	83	5	20	14	–3	15	15
Kombolcha	88	5	9	6	3	2	5
Mekele	82	11	14	12	3	4	17
Dire Dawa	92	5	2	3	5	4	9
Harar	87	12	7	10	5	4	9
Subtotal	85	9	12	12	2	9	55
Central							
Addis Ababa	94	5	5	9	1	7	37
Total	82	14	15	14	2	9	178

Source: Author's survey, 1996.

consequently less, as small as 63 percent and 65 percent, respectively, of the sale price in Nekempte and Bure. In terminal markets the results suggest that local procurement is important and that transport costs are significantly lower. Consequently, the share of the sale price attributed to purchase price is as high as 94 percent and 92 percent, respectively, in Addis Ababa and Dire Dawa.

Markets for relatively undifferentiated goods, such as agricultural commodities, are expected to be less risky, with greater competition and low profit margins. The very low actual profit rates of 2 percent for the sample as a whole confirm that this may indeed be the case in the Ethiopian grain market (Table 3.8). At the same time, profit rates vary considerably between and within markets, with very high coefficients of variations for both the market averages and the averages by type of market. In the surplus areas, profits appear to be very low, and even negative in the case of markets in western Wellega and Arsi, while they are relatively high in the Gojam area. Profit rates vary less among traders and among markets in the deficit markets with the exception of Dessie, where average profit rates are negative and highly variable. Finally, in Addis Ababa profit rates are very low, which is to be expected in that traders typically buy and sell in the same market and marketed volumes are generally much larger than in other markets.

Annual Sales and Gross Profits

Annual sales revenue is calculated using data collected on annual quantities purchased and sold as well as price data. As shown in Table 3.9, traders in Assela and Addis Ababa have the highest average annual sales in tons, with roughly 1,100 tons sold per trader. Taking into account the number of traders per market, Bahir Dar has the second highest volume of trade in the sample, following Addis Ababa.

Applying the average profit rate for the sample of 2 percent to calculate gross annual profits for all markets corrects for the potential bias that arises from using the profit rate obtained for the most recent transaction. Following the pattern of annual sales, gross annual profits per trading firm were highest in

Table 3.9 Annual sales and gross profits by type of market, 1996

Type of market		Annual sales (tons)	Annual gross sales revenue (Eth. Birr)[a]	Annual gross sales revenue (US$)	Annual gross profit (US$)
Surplus					
Nekempte	Mean	237	302,063	47,569	951
(*N* = 9)	SD	237	329,769	51,932	1,039
Jaji	Mean	218	307,159	48,371	967
(*N* = 4)	SD	241	386,706	60,899	1,218
Assela	Mean	1,111	1,595,209	251,214	5,024
(*N* = 7)	SD	1,742	2,472,088	389,305	7,786
Sagure	Mean	286	394,026	62,051	1,241
(*N* = 5)	SD	237	339,874	53,523	1,070
Bahir Dar	Mean	352	468,789	73,825	1,476
(*N* = 30)	SD	455	642,650	101,205	2,024
Bure	Mean	330	428,167	67,428	1,349
(*N* = 9)	SD	400	599,122	94,350	1,887
Subtotal	Mean	404	546,890	86,124	1,722
(*N* = 64)	SD	702	993,514	156,459	3,129
Deficit					
Dessie	Mean	163	164,680	25,934	519
(*N* = 14)	SD	170	153,312	24,144	483
Kombolcha	Mean	348	499,826	78,713	1,574
(*N* = 5)	SD	564	790,905	124,552	2,491
Mekele	Mean	106	179,515	28,270	565
(*N* = 13)	SD	50	85,524	13,468	269
Dire Dawa	Mean	108	158,850	25,016	500
(*N* = 9)	SD	60	109,345	17,220	344
Harar	Mean	375	500,053	78,748	1,575
(*N* = 9)	SD	384	581,006	91,497	1,830
Subtotal	Mean	193	261,369	41,160	823
(*N* = 48)	SD	265	372,560	58,671	1,173
Central					
Addis Ababa	Mean	1,112	1,703,018	268,192	5,364
(*N* = 37)	SD	1,797	3,070,966	483,617	9,672
Total	Mean	509	735,636	115,848	2,317
(*N* = 151)	SD	1,067	1,744,799	274,772	5,495

Source: Author's survey, 1996.

[a] Eth. Birr 6.35 = US$1 in 1995/96.

Assela and Addis Ababa, US$5,000 and US$5,400, respectively (Table 3.9). For the sample as a whole, the average annual firm profit was US$2,300. It is important to note that this figure represents gross profits in that it does not account for the fixed costs of warehouse rental, employee salaries, interest costs, taxes, or other fixed costs. The residual profits after deduction of these costs would represent the returns relative to managerial inputs.

With the exception of Assela and Addis Ababa, gross annual profits varied between US$500 in Dire Dawa and US$1,575 in Harar (Table 3.9). Moreover, high coefficients of variation for the market averages suggest that gross profits varied between traders and were linked to the size of the firm, the size of the firm's working capital, and the extent of the firm's specialization in grain trade.

Breakdown of Marketing Costs

The traders surveyed were asked to identify for their most recent completed wholesale transaction all the costs incurred between the purchase and the sale of the grain, including up to 20 types of physical marketing costs. These marketing costs were variable in that they were specific to the transaction rather than fixed costs for things such as warehouse

Table 3.10 Breakdown of marketing costs by type of market, 1996

Type of market		Percent for handling	Percent for sacking	Percent for transport	Percent for storage	Percent for road stops	Percent for brokers	Percent for travel	Percent for tips/other	Total percent
Surplus										
Nekempte	Mean (SD)	8 (6)	3 (3)	52 (25)	0 (1)	8 (6)	7 (3)	2 (3)	2 (4)	100
	N	18	18	18	18	18	15	18	18	15
Jaji	Mean (SD)	8 (3)	6 (2)	53 (11)	0 (0)	18 (4)	6 (3)	1 (3)	7 (13)	100
	N	8	8	8	8	8	8	8	8	8
Assela	Mean (SD)	7 (3)	4 (4)	55 (5)	0 (1)	27 (4)	5 (3)	2 (2)	1 (1)	100
	N	12	12	12	14	12	12	14	13	12
Sagure	Mean (SD)	6 (3)	4 (4)	49 (21)	0 (1)	17 (14)	6 (4)	1 (3)	1 (2)	100
	N	8	8	8	10	9	7	9	9	7
Bahir Dar	Mean (SD)	9 (15)	3 (7)	45 (35)	0 (1)	4 (12)	7 (18)	1 (3)	5 (13)	100
	N	49	54	49	58	49	36	52	55	36
Bure	Mean (SD)	7 (7)	9 (12)	45 (29)	0 (0)	6 (6)	2 (2)	1 (3)	4 (8)	100
	N	15	15	16	18	16	12	18	16	12
Subtotal	Mean (SD)	8 (11)	4 (7)	48 (28)	0 (1)	10 (12)	6 (11)	1 (3)	4 (10)	100
	N	110	115	111	126	112	90	119	124	90
Deficit										
Dessie	Mean (SD)	12 (20)	6 (7)	52 (26)	0 (2)	2 (2)	8 (4)	0 (0)	4 (12)	100
	N	17	17	17	27	21	15	25	25	15
Kombolcha	Mean (SD)	19 (16)	2 (4)	62 (7)	0 (0)	1 (2)	7 (6)	0 (0)	4 (8)	100
	N	5	6	5	8	7	5	9	7	5
Mekele	Mean (SD)	8 (11)	8 (21)	32 (35)	0 (0)	5 (8)	15 (29)	2 (4)	3 (10)	100
	N	23	27	27	26	28	18	28	27	18
Dire Dawa	Mean (SD)	40 (39)	20 (26)	4 (16)	0 (0)	1 (4)	2 (7)	0 (0)	4 (17)	100
	N	12	12	18	18	18	9	18	18	9
Harar	Mean (SD)	50 (39)	13 (15)	18 (31)	0 (1)	3 (8)	10 (13)	0 (1)	0 (2)	100
	N	9	9	11	18	11	9	18	18	9
Subtotal	Mean (SD)	22 (29)	10 (18)	30 (33)	0 (1)	3 (6)	10 (18)	1 (2)	3 (11)	100
	N	66	71	78	97	85	56	98	95	56
Central										
Addis Ababa	Mean (SD)	34 (36)	15 (23)	5 (17)	0 (2)	1 (5)	9 (25)	0 (0)	11 (25)	100
	N	46	45	67	69	72	38	72	71	38
Total	Mean (SD)	18 (26)	8 (16)	31 (33)	0 (1)	5 (9)	8 (17)	1 (2)	5 (16)	100
N		222	231	256	292	269	184	289	294	184

Source: Author's survey, 1996.

rental, employee wages, and so on. For the purposes of analysis, the costs were reclassified into eight categories (Table 3.10). Handling costs comprise the costs of loading the grain at the time of purchase, off-loading it at the trader's warehouse, loading it to a transport vehicle for sale, and off-loading it at the site of sale. Sacking costs include the costs of empty sacks (taking into account the multiple uses of the same sacks) and the cost of sewing the tops of the sacks. Transport costs include the costs of transporting the grain from the place of purchase to the trader's warehouse and transporting it from the trader's warehouse to the place of sale. Storage costs refer to the variable costs per sack of temporarily storing the grain either in a private warehouse or in the broker's warehouse between purchase and sale. Kella costs are composed of payments at road stops during the course of transport from the place of purchase to the trader's warehouse and from the trader's warehouse to the place of sale. Broker costs include the commissions paid to agents or brokers for either the purchase or the sale of goods, as well as the commissions paid to transport brokers for finding transport services. Travel costs refer to the costs incurred by the trader in accompanying a shipment, including the costs of personal travel as well as accommodation at the distant market town. Finally, the category of costs called "Tips and other" includes tips paid during the purchase and sale, as well as other costs related to storage or transport losses, phytosanitary measures, and others. Notable omissions from these costs are those imposed by taxes and other regulations. This omission was made because, unlike taxes in other countries, Ethiopian taxes were not variable fees incurred during the course of the market day, but rather were paid annually.

Among the various costs, transport costs appear to be the most important; for the surveyed transactions they ranged between 45 percent and 62 percent of total marketing costs for most of the regional markets with the exception of Dire Dawa and Harar (Table 3.10). Because of the relative lack of transport activities by traders in the central market as well as in these two markets, the sample average was 31 percent. As noted earlier, the main value added in the Ethiopian grain marketing chain is that added in the spatial transfer of goods. Thus, it is to be expected that transport costs represent the bulk of marketing costs. However, adding the costs of road stops to the transport costs increased the percentage of transport-related costs for traders in the regional markets to as high as 82 percent in Assela, 71 percent in Jaji, and 58 percent for the surplus markets as a whole. Kella costs, which can act as a disincentive for trade, appear to have been considerably higher in Wellega (8 to 18 percent) and Arsi (17 to 27 percent) compared to the other zones. The higher kella costs explain the negative profits or very low profits noted for the markets in these areas.

The second most important costs are those of handling, which ranged from 8 percent to 19 percent in the markets in which significant transport activities occurred and considerably more in markets in which transport was limited (Table 3.10), such as Addis Ababa (34 percent), Dire Dawa (40 percent), and Harar (50 percent). Overall, handling costs for the sample represented 18 percent of the total marketing costs. Adding sacking costs to the costs of handling results in a combined share of handling-related costs of 26 percent for the sample. This is a very significant finding in that these costs are directly linked to the inefficiency built into trading practices. First, loading and off-loading are labor-intensive, sack-specific activities, the costs of which would be significantly reduced by making bulk shipments rather than selling grain by the sack. Second, the lack of a system for grading and standardizing grain requires the visual inspection of the grain, sack by sack, resulting in the need to resack every sack of grain at the time of sale. Thus, for every transaction a new sack must be purchased, handling costs must be incurred in off-loading and transferring the grain to new sacks, and the sacks must be sewn. This involves not only labor costs but also time costs, resulting in the slowing of transactions.

The third most important cost category is that of commissions paid for brokerage services. These costs, which represent the costs of market coordination, ranged from 6 to 10 percent of the total marketing costs for the three types of markets in the sample, 8 percent overall (Table 3.10). This is an interesting finding, because market coordination services appear to be equally important even where trade does not occur across long distances, such as in the central market, where broker fees represent 9 percent of costs. The following chapter explores the range of services provided by a broker in exchange for this fee and the nature of the brokerage institution in greater detail in the following chapter. However, the importance of this institution is confirmed by its relatively high share of the marketing costs and by its pervasive use in all the markets studied.

Finally, it is noteworthy that the share of costs related to personal travel by traders accompanying shipments was rather small, only 1 percent of total costs (Table 3.10). This is in stark contrast to recent findings in Malawi and Benin, where personal travel accounted for 23 and 11 percent of costs, respectively. Given that brokers play a much less significant role in the market in those countries than in Ethiopia, this finding can be interpreted as an indication that the presence of brokers in the Ethiopian context reduces the search costs that would be incurred by traders who would need to personally accompany their shipments. Subsequent chapters rigorously test this interpretation.

Summary

Analysis of traders' operations and their arbitrage behavior reveals that Ethiopian grain wholesaler trading firms are generally small-scale, personalized enterprises in which the owner is the sole owner and dominant player in the business. In 70 percent of cases, owners are also managers. Manager-owners appear to be well educated relative to the general population, with 10 years of schooling, and are predominantly male. On average, traders have had 10 years of business experience, often starting out in businesses other than those they currently operate. Firms are not bought or sold, but are typically started up by their current owners, indicating that a firm's reputation is not separate from its owner's. Social capital plays an important part in trade in that at least half of the traders interviewed are children of current or past traders, generally their fathers.

Further, with the exception of Addis Ababa, the grain trade operations sampled do not appear to be highly specialized in wholesale activity, despite their identification as wholesalers. Thus, in surplus areas wholesalers are also engaged in assembling grain by purchasing it directly from farmers. In deficit areas the converse is true, with wholesalers engaged in selling grain in smaller quantities to retailers and directly to consumers. In addition, businesses do not appear to be fully specialized in grain trading, with 34 percent indicating that they are engaged in other types of trade or income-earning activities.

Trade enterprises are characterized by a very low asset base. Only 6 percent of the sample own transport vehicles, and more than 70 percent rent storage space. Traders invest relatively little in business assets outside of scales. Surprisingly, a relatively high proportion of traders own telephones and have electricity. In terms of financial assets, only one-third of the sample obtained formal bank loans during the survey year, although all traders indicated that they had access to other sources of credit, at less favorable terms. Despite the lack of access to formal credit, traders appear to be well endowed in terms of total loan amounts (US$14,000 per year on average) and working capital levels (roughly US$9,000).

Due to the regional disparities in marketable surplus of specific grains, grain trade in Ethiopia is characterized by long-distance wholesale shipments, ranging from 200 to 1,200 kilometers. Spatial flows of grain conform to a radial configuration in which grain is shipped from western, northern, and southern surplus-producing areas to the central market of Addis Ababa. From Addis Ababa grain flows outward to the deficit areas in the northern parts of the country, as well as to eastern and southeastern markets. Although Addis Ababa is the main hub of the spatial configuration of markets, smaller hubs are emerging, such as Nazareth. Dire Dawa and Harar appear to function as terminal markets, with little transport activity by local traders. Bahir Dar in the Gojam area appears to be another emerging market hub. In this area new marketing channels are evolving, with traders bypassing the Addis Ababa market and shipping grain directly along new or revitalized roads to Wello, Tigray, and neighboring Eritrea.

Traders' arbitrage behavior is mainly limited to transport, or transformation over space, with the exception of the terminal markets of Addis Ababa as well as Dire Dawa and Harar. In these terminal markets arbitrage activity is very restricted: traders buy grain from regional sellers, then turn around and sell it to urban buyers. The average distance traveled by the traders surveyed for transactions was 200 kilometers. Overall, their marketing costs represented 83 percent of their gross margins, indicating that traders are not achieving very large profits. The proportion of marketing costs represented by marketing margins is quite variable, however, with very high marketing costs in the regional markets compared to the terminal markets.

There is also a high degree of variability in the level of absolute profits among the various markets. Thus, profits appear to be significantly higher in the Gojam markets of Bahir Dar and Bure, possibly due to new and potentially riskier market channels. As expected, the large number of traders and the limited services provided lead to very low profits in the Addis Ababa market, where traders appear to benefit mainly from a high volume of operations rather than from large profit margins. In relative terms, the costs of purchasing grain represents 82 percent of its sale price, while marketing costs and profits represent 16 percent and 2 percent, respectively. The very low share of profits, indicative of low returns to trade, suggests that trade is quite competitive in general, although this rate varies considerably between markets and between traders. This finding seems inconsistent with hypotheses that grain trade is a highly risky activity, due in part to the high differentiation of individual types of grains. This may be because of the presence of brokers, who play a critical role in reducing the risk of contract failure and in inspecting and certifying the various qualities of grains in the market, as subsequent chapters explore.

CHAPTER 4

The Middlemen of the Middlemen: The Institution of Brokers

The geographic dispersion of trade, the absence of grades and standards, the lack of market information, and limited legal enforcement are factors that contribute to an increased risk of commitment failure, which is the failure to complete a transaction. In the absence of formal means to mitigate the risk of commitment failure, how do Ethiopian grain traders carry out long-distance transactions? One option employed by traders is personalized exchange, whereby they trade grain only with partners whom they know and trust, who may be associated to them by kinship, religion, or ethnicity. Alternatively, survey evidence reveals that traders use the services of brokers to conduct long-distance trade with anonymous partners.

This chapter closely examines the institution of brokerage in the Ethiopian grain market. It explores the sources of commitment failure in the Ethiopian market, then engages in an empirical examination of the structure of the brokerage institution. The chapter then addresses how brokers enable traders to reduce commitment failure.

The analysis of brokerage in this chapter relies on primary data collected in 1996 in a formal survey of central market brokers located in Addis Ababa. The sample included 17 brokers randomly selected from a total population of 40 established brokers in the central market. The main purpose of the survey was to obtain a fuller understanding of how brokers operate as well as to corroborate the information provided in the trader survey, described in the previous chapter. The broker survey covered the function and operations of brokers, as well as their assets, resources, transaction costs, and social capital.

Sources of Commitment Failure in the Ethiopian Market

As in many other developing economies in sub-Saharan Africa and elsewhere, traders in the liberalized Ethiopian grain market operate in a context in which grain prices are not publicly announced, grain is highly differentiated because there is no formal standardization and classification system, contracts are oral and nonstandardized, grain shipments are not inspected or certified officially, and there are very limited means of legally enforcing contracts (Dadi, Negassa, and Franzel 1992; Kuawab Business Consultants 1994). These constraints cause grain traders to be highly vulnerable to being cheated with respect to market prices, quality and quantity of the delivered grain, and other contractual terms such as the timing of delivery and grain spoilage or loss during transport, inter alia. The traders interviewed reported that partners can, and do, cheat by delivering lower-quality grain than was discussed at the time of sale. Since there are no official inspections of grain, a trader who contacts a partner by telephone is forced to take the partner's word at face value. Furthermore, grain quality can deteriorate in the course of storage or transport to the buyer. The relevant parameters of quality for Ethiopian grain are qualitative and open to considerably different interpretations. Traders can deceive partners by misquoting or omitting information on any of these parameters at the time of the oral agreement regarding the grain price.

Other opportunities for fraud are presented by the lack of standardized sacks. Traders indicate that sacks, which are reused numerous times, vary dramatically in terms of the quantity of grain they will hold and their quality. Sellers can cheat by using sacks that hold less than the 100 kilograms that they are presumed to hold. In small rural markets where there are no scales, buyers are reported to cheat farmers routinely by putting grain in sacks that hold considerably more than 100 kilograms. Moreover, the practice of reusing sacks creates room for opportunistic behavior. Traders report that buying a load of grain in the sacks of a selling merchant is undesirable, because the seller is likely to provide the oldest possible sacks, which are likely to tear and cause grain loss or damage over the course of transport.

The commitment problem is also a function of the point at which ownership of grain is transferred between partners. When a seller retains ownership of, and concomitant risk for, a shipment of grain until it reaches its final destination, the trader is highly vulnerable to the buyer's reneging on his agreement to buy. Similarly, if the buyer takes ownership of a load of grain at the seller's venue, the buyer is highly vulnerable to fraudulent representation of the grain or damage during transport.

In the event that cheating occurs, recourse to a legal third party is very limited in Ethiopia. In part, the lack of legal recourse is due to the time-consuming nature and inaccessibility of formal courts. Moreover, as elsewhere in Africa, it is not customary for business partners to engage in legal suits (Berry 1993). Platteau (1994b) argues that markets depend on generalized social norms rather than continuous legal sanctions. According to the traders interviewed, a trader who has been deceived by a partner must return to the market in order to seek out the wrongdoer and engage in a public confrontation. When the partner is not found or a settlement cannot be reached, the trader bears the loss. This commitment problem severely inhibits traders from placing orders with other traders in distant markets or, in general, from trading with unknown merchants, even if they meet face to face.

The Structure of Grain Brokerage

Brokers generally do not trade on their own account, with less than 10 percent of transactions made for themselves. However, although they do not bear market price risk, they are held accountable in the event of a breach of contract. Brokers are permanently located in the central market and thus are easily identifiable to all traders who come in and out of the market. Their permanent presence in the central market is a mechanism that ensures the transmission of information on traders' reputations. In addition, their continuous presence implies that in the event that a falling-out between partners engaged in long-distance trade, a broker can be contacted to mediate and resolve the dispute.

Characteristics of Brokers

The 1996 survey revealed that brokers are similar to the larger group of traders in terms of age, educational level, religion, and gender (Table 4.1). However, brokers appear to be considerably better endowed than traders

Table 4.1 Comparison of brokers and traders, 1996

	Brokers (N = 17)		Traders (N = 152)	
	Mean	SD	Mean	SD
Demographic measure				
Age (years)	36.21	11.49	32.83	12.32
Education (years)	8.29	4.41	9.61	3.64
Religion: Orthodox Christian (percent)[a]	78.6	...	66.4	...
Gender: Male (percent)	100.0	...	94.1	...
Years in grain trade	8.77	7.63	10.41	8.76
Assets				
Working capital (Ethiopian birr)[b]	79,750	100,805	55,184	62,647
Warehouse capacity (tons)[c]	92.89	75.80	115.55	171.08
Vehicle (percent)	28.6	...	5.9	...
Telephone service (percent)[c]	71.4	...	38.8	...
Social capital				
Number of friends in trade[d]	4.60	5.89	6.17	8.74
Number of family members in trade	1.20	1.69	0.83	1.38
Number of local contacts	15.50	13.46	4.59	4.32
Number of distant contacts	38.50	19.50	7.89	7.46
Number of markets in which operate	5.80	2.70	3.46	2.86
Father in grain trade (percent)	60.0	...	48.4	...
Search behavior				
Minutes spent daily in information gathering	37.80	41.93	39.06	39.79
Number of people consulted daily	7.80	8.43	4.24	3.28
Number of employees engaged in searching	5.00	3.89	1.74	1.29
Number of weekly transactions	20.00	17.04	1.56	0.74

Source: Author's survey, 1996.

Note: No standard deviation is reported for percentages.
[a] If not Orthodox, religion is generally Muslim.
[b] Eth. Birr 6.35 = US$1 in 1996.
[c] The sum of rented and owned storage capacity.
[d] Friends are defined as personal contacts who are not merely acquaintances.

with working capital, vehicles and telephones. Thus, they have 44 percent more working capital than traders and 29 percent of brokers own vehicles in contrast to only 6 percent of traders. Similarly, 71 percent of brokers have telephones compared to 39 percent of traders (Table 3.7). This comparison suggests that established brokers are relatively well off, with greater access to financial resources. It also suggests that brokers may be involved in a number of activities outside of direct brokerage, such as providing transport services, extending loans to clients, and engaging in grain trading on their own account. Brokers are highly heterogeneous with respect to working capital, implying that brokers may perform different market roles, according to their capacities.

Brokers are also better endowed with social capital than are traders. It is interesting to note that while brokers and traders have similar endowments of "in-born" social capital, such as family and friends in grain trade,[9] brokers have considerably more "acquired" social capital, with three times more local contacts and nearly five times more distant trading contacts (Table 4.1).

In terms of their search capacity, brokers are clearly more search-efficient than traders in that although they spend roughly the same amount of time in information gathering as traders, they consult with nearly twice as

[9] Two types of social capital can be distinguished: "in-born" social capital that is obtained by an individual involuntarily, such as family connections, ethnic or religion-based networks, and "acquired" social capital that is based on the individual's choice to join an association, invest in contacts, and so on (Fafchamps and Minten 1999).

Table 4.2 Brokers' operations, 1996

	Mean	Coefficient variation
Total number of clients	60.50	0.53
Number of local buyer clients	11.20	1.41
Number of distant buyer clients	7.44	0.96
Number of local seller clients	2.10	2.56
Number of distant seller clients	38.44	0.45
Share of distant buyer clients with whom broker can work solely by telephone	19.63	1.89
Share of distant seller clients with whom broker can work solely by telephone	76.77	0.47
Share of buyer clients to whom broker would offer buyer credit	32.22	1.07
Share of seller clients to whom broker would offer sales advance	41.15	1.06
Weekly transactions (100-kg bags)		
January 1996	2,777.27	0.76
February 1996	2,788.64	0.82
March 1996	2,543.18	0.82
April 1996	1,411.36	0.98
May 1996	1,752.27	1.06
June 1996	1,956.82	0.85

Source: Author's survey, 1996.

Note: $N = 17$.

many people, have three times more employees engaged in search activities, and conduct more than 10 times as many transactions as do traders (Table 4.1).

Brokers' Operations

Grain brokers operate from permanent market stalls in the central grain market, known as the Ehil Berenda, in Addis Ababa. Each broker handles transactions for clients in nearly six markets, on average, with a total of 60 clients (Table 4.2). Of these clients, most are distant sellers; on average a broker may have 38 such clients. There is relatively little variation among brokers in terms of the total number of clients and the number of clients in distant markets. However, there is more variation in the number of local clients, indicating that some brokers may be more specialized than others in handling distant orders.

Brokers who work with clients outside of the central market may handle orders exclusively by telephone, indicating the sophistication of the brokerage service as well as the degree of trust between brokers and traders. The data reveal that brokers work solely by telephone with more seller clients, 77 percent, than with buyer clients, 20 percent (Table 4.2). Underlying reasons for this difference in behavior may be the greater risks involved for buyers, who are more likely to be cheated on the quality or price of the grain that they order.

Over the six-month period from January through June 1996, the average amount of grain handled weekly by each broker ranged from 141 tons to 279 tons. Extrapolating these figures for the estimated 40 established brokers operating in the market allows one to assume that approximately 423,000 tons of grain were handled by the established Addis Ababa brokers in the 1995–96 marketing year.[10] In relative terms, this amounts to only 16 percent of the total marketable surplus of grain in 1995/96, estimated at 2.6 million tons. However, considering that only 1.2 million tons were marketed through assemblers and wholesalers, the share handled by brokers was actually 52 percent of the grain marketed through traders.

[10] Lirenso (1993) estimates that in 1992 some 342 regional wholesalers from 64 market towns shipped 1,354 tons weekly to 50 brokers.

Functions of Brokers

Due to the constraints noted earlier, the Ethiopian grain market is primarily, if not entirely, a physical cash market. Thus, not only are there no forward transactions, but all transactions involve visually inspecting and entire shipment of grain rather than a sample. In this context, brokers' functions involve five distinct activities, some of which could otherwise be considered "public goods": providing market information to clients, arranging the handling and logistics of grain delivery, grading and classifying grain, determining its market price, and matching buyers and sellers. Of these, the latter two functions are typically the ones most closely associated with brokers in most world markets, where the function of brokers is generally considerably narrower than that of Ethiopian brokers.

Ethiopian grain brokers also consider their role as "witnesses" of transactions the most important service they provide. That is, in facilitating transactions between buyers and sellers, brokers, by their presence and the weight of their reputation, sanction the legitimacy of their clients. In the event of a dispute, a broker can be called upon to enforce the contract or mediate a negotiated settlement.

Brokers provide market information and business advice to clients on a continuous basis. After consulting with a broker about prevailing market conditions and prices, a seller in a distant market will send a shipment of grain directly to the broker, in effect placing a sale order, or a buyer will place a purchase order, which involves sending funds to the broker. In each case, the buyer or seller assumes the total burden of price risk in the transaction and faces the transaction costs of holding either grain inventory or physical cash fixed during the search period.

In the case of a sale order, the broker physically receives the shipment of grain on his premises. Generally the grain is not off-loaded from the transport vehicle, which remains parked in front of the broker's stall where it is visible to incoming buyers. After receiving a grain shipment, the broker inspects and grades the incoming grain. In order to ascertain the quality of the grain, the broker uses a pointed tubular device, known as a *memermeria,* to take samples randomly from different sacks of the shipment. On the basis of this type of inspection of the grain, brokers set the market price for each of the types of grain they receive. Each broker sets an average of seven different prices daily. The time required for brokers to set prices ranges between 15 and 30 minutes, or about 6 minutes per commodity (Table 4.2).

The search for buyers or sellers involves discussing the state of the market with other brokers, touring the marketplace by foot talking to traders, placing phone calls to interested parties, and instructing assistants to stand on top of trucks shouting out the available types and qualities of grain. At the point of sale or purchase, the broker arranges the handling of the grain and the transport logistics.

When a sale is completed on behalf of a client, a broker deducts the commission and remits the funds to the regional seller. If the grain has not been sold and the seller is short of funds, the broker may extend a sales advance to a valued client. Brokers indicated that they provide this service to roughly 40 percent of their clientele (Table 4.2). Unsold grain is off-loaded to the broker's warehouse, where it is stored for a monthly rental fee. Depending on the relationship with a client, the broker may also provide buyer credit for up to 30 days. Brokers offer this service to approximately one-third of all their clients (Table 4.2).

Price Discovery by Brokers

Price discovery generally refers to the process by which a market-clearing price is obtained in a centralized market.[11] In Ethiopia, grain brokers carry out an implicit bidding

[11] See Chicago Board of Trade (1989).

Table 4.3 Price discovery by brokers, 1996

	Percentage of brokers
Existence of single daily market price	78.6
Frequency of price changes	
Daily	21.4
2–3 times per day	64.3
	Mean (SD)
Time required to set market prices (minutes)	18.77 (11.25)
Number of prices set daily	7.30 (3.47)
Time required to set each price	6.20 (4.80)

Source: Author's survey, 1996.

Note: $N = 17$.

process that results in a single daily Addis Ababa spot price for each type and origin of grain prevailing in the Addis Ababa market. Before the start of the market day at 6 A.M., brokers individually evaluate the supply and demand conditions in the market. Using the previous day's closing price as a starting basis, brokers individually "fix" a market price for each type and quality of grain they have received from regional clients. They then adjust this price according to what other brokers may have fixed in nearby stalls. It takes some 18 minutes, on average, for this *tâtonnement* process to result in a single daily spot price for each grain, by type, region of origin, and quality.

For this reason, contrary to what is seen in many agricultural markets throughout Africa, a single cash price prevails in the Addis Ababa market for a given quality and origin of a particular grain. This spot price generally holds for the entire trading period (between 6 and 9 A.M.) or changes one or two times as the closing of the market approaches at 9 A.M.[12] On a given day, brokers determine up to 40 such spot prices for the five principal grains traded on the Addis Ababa market: teff, wheat, maize, barley, and sorghum (Table 4.3).

This price discovery process has significant implications for the national grain economy in that studies of market integration have shown that prices in major regional deficit and surplus markets are closely linked to the Addis Ababa price (Negassa 1998; Dercon 1995). The price discovery role played by brokers represents a highly specialized market function, resulting in finite variations in prices according to very precisely defined qualities of grain. The relevant parameters of quality used by brokers are color, taste, appearance, moisture content, impurity, breakage of kernels, and baking qualities.[13] Thus, on a given market day 11 different prices of wheat, varying from Eth. Birr 105 to 175 per bag, were noted in the Addis Ababa market, each of which was precisely identified according to its region of origin, variety, and grade (Table 4.4). Similarly, teff prices ranged from Eth. Birr 130 to 245, and barley prices from Eth. Birr 105 to 300 per bag.

Surprisingly, official trading agencies do not recognize the price discovery function of brokers, and trade licensing and regulatory bodies neither distinguish brokers from wholesale traders nor acknowledge their price discovery role. Moreover, this function is equally hidden from other market participants, such as consumers and farmers, because the various grades of grain determined by brokers are not openly labeled or known. Due to this lack of transparency, a recent attempt to establish a public market information system, set up to report a single price for each of the five grains, failed to distinguish the origins and qualities of grains, as is done by brokers (Grain Market Research Project 1996).[14] This failure was due to the lack of awareness of this relatively sophisticated market function of brokers.

In essence, the Ethiopian price discovery process most closely resembles what is known

[12] The Addis Ababa grain-trading association established that trading would be done only between 6 and 9 A.M. Monday through Saturday. Other rules set by the association concern the logistics of delivery trucks and market taxes for infrastructural improvement.

[13] Brokers revealed in interviews that they use these parameters to determine appropriate prices.

[14] The grain prices reported were for mixed teff, white barley, white wheat, white sorghum, and maize.

as ring trading in the London metals market, in which metals brokers determine the daily price of each metal within a preset time frame through bidding on the price (Gibson-Jarvie 1983). Other examples are found in the London bullion market, which informally determines the London Gold Fix, a daily gold price.[15]

Entry into Brokerage

There do not appear to be significant formal barriers to becoming a broker. Indeed, as noted earlier, there are no official requirements for or restrictions on becoming a broker that are distinct from those one needs to obtain a trading license. Yet the number of brokers is relatively small in the Addis Ababa market. Given the relatively lucrative opportunities and the lower risk involved in brokerage compared to wholesale trade, what, if any, are the informal barriers to entry?

Brokers themselves perceive the trust (*imnet*) they acquire from their network of traders as a critical asset in their business, and lack of such trust as the principal barrier to entry into brokerage. How do brokers acquire trust? One means is through inherited social capital. Thus, 60 percent of the brokers surveyed had a parent in grain trade, and 40 percent had a parent in grain brokerage. Grain brokerage businesses pass from generation to generation, gradually transferring trust from father to son, who acquires the father's clients. The high value placed on an Ethiopian broker's work is similar to the importance, in traditional Chinese trading practices in southeast Asia, of *xinyong,* or trust, which is also transferred across generations (Menkoff 1994).[16]

Another means by which brokers secure the loyalty of their clients is through extending sales advances and buyer credits, which potentially requires that brokers dispose of a certain amount of working capital for these purposes and also that brokers be willing to be exposed to some risk. Traders are exposed to price risk when they send grain shipments to their brokers without locking in a price, but brokers must be willing to assume the counterparty risk associated with lending funds to their clients. As noted earlier, brokers

Table 4.4 Wholesale grain prices in the Addis Ababa market, December 1996

Grain	Origin	Variety	Quality (grade)	Price (Eth. Birr[a]/100 kg bag[b])
Teff	Ada	Magna	1st	245
	Ada	Red	1st	165
	Butajira	White	1st	215
	Welenkomi	Mixed	1st	180
	Gojjam	Mixed	1st	155
	Gojjam	Abolsey	3rd	140
	Gojjam	Red	1st	130
Wheat	Ada	Israel	1st	175
	Ada	Israel	2nd	150
	Ada	White	1st	n.a.[c]
	Ada	White	2nd	160
	Ada	Aybo	1st	175
	Ada	Abesha	1st	175
	Ada	Abesha	2nd	170
	Arsi	Favel	1st	145
	Arsi	Favel	2nd	135
	Arsi	Favel	3rd	105
	Arsi	Dashin	2nd	135
	Bale	Favel	1st	140
Maize	Bale	Red	1st	87
	Gojjam	White	1st	85
	Gojjam	Red	2nd	70
	Illubabor	White	2nd	65
Sorghum	Wellega	White	1st	140
	Jirru	White	1st	140
	Jirru	Yellow	1st	130
	Arsi	Red	1st	110
Barley	Sodo	Senef	1st	300
	Sodo	Senef	2nd	260
	Sodo	Wegertena	1st	225
	Arsi	Birra	2nd	160
	Arsi	Black	2nd	130
	Arsi	Asharo	2nd	105
	Guder	Black	2nd	135
	Guder	Asharro	1st	125

Source: Author's survey, 1996.
[a] Eth. Birr 6.35 = US$1 in 1996.
[b] Bags are unstandardized and vary in capacity between 90 and 120 kg.
[c] Price undetermined during survey.

[15] These insights were provided by Jeffrey Williams.

[16] The existence of trust is most frequently cited by Chinese traders to explain their success in business. The need "to trust trust" is among the safeguards against the possible breach of business commitments (see Menkoff 1994; Fukuyama 1995).

Table 4.5 Traders' rationale for choice of brokers' services, 1996

Reasons to work with broker[a]	Percent traders	Reasons not to work with broker[b]	Percent traders
Broker has better access to market information	24.8	I trade with partners whom I know well	25.9
Broker acts as guarantor	9.7	I know the market well enough	52.8
Broker has more contacts	38.9	Brokers cheat on prices	6.5
Broker identifies good quality	8.0	I want to save commission fees	9.3
I have no choice	10.6	I don't need a quick transaction	4.6
Broker gives business advice	1.8	Disagreement with broker	0.9
Less costly to work with broker	6.2		

Source: Author's survey, 1996.

[a] $N = 113$.

[b] $N = 108$.

are significantly better endowed with working capital than are traders, indicating that inadequate liquidity may represent a critical barrier to entry into brokerage.

Poor location also plays a role in limiting entry into brokerage. That is, an important aspect of brokerage is being physically present in the market, with a fixed place of business and storage facilities. The number of stalls in the Addis Ababa grain market is limited. This may restrict the number of brokers who can operate in this market. This is analogous to the fixed number of brokers' seats in formal exchanges, resulting in a secondary market for the seats themselves.

The Role of Brokers in Reducing Commitment Failure

The likelihood of commitment failure causes traders to be extremely reluctant to trade with partners they don't know. It could be expected that exchange between unknown long-distance partners would occur rarely because traders would anticipate cheating by their partners. Yet there is ample evidence that grain is traded over considerable distances around Ethiopia and that cheating is the exception rather than the rule. The reason is because there are brokers to limit the risks of commitment failure.

How do brokers resolve the commitment problem? First, as neutral intermediaries, brokers are uniquely able to gather information from a large number of traders. The traders surveyed asserted that their primary reasons for using brokers were the brokers' access to traders and their superior market information (Table 4.5). Close to 40 percent of traders cited brokers' access to more contacts as the most important reason for their choice, while 25 percent listed the brokers' access to information as most important. Conversely, when traders feel they know the market or have sufficiently trustworthy partners, they don't use brokers. More than half of the traders interviewed (53 percent) noted that if they had felt they knew the market well enough, they would not have used brokers, while 26 percent indicated that brokers were unnecessary when they had well-known trading partners.

Second, brokers are perceived as the guarantors or underwriters of given transactions. Brokers indicate that they see their role as guarantors or witnesses as their most important function in the market. Through their mediation they ensure that *imnet* is present in long-distance transactions.

Third, because brokers are permanently located in the central market they are easily identifiable by all traders who come in and out of the market. Thus, they are natural repositories of information regarding market flows, the behavior of market participants, and the outcomes of past transactions. Their permanent presence in the central market provides a mechanism for the transmission of information on traders' reputations. In addition, their continuous presence implies that in the event of a falling-out between partners in long-distance trade, the broker can be contacted to mediate and resolve the dispute.

Summary

The effective expansion of the grain market depends in part on the ability of traders to exchange grain anonymously with buyers and sellers in distant markets without risk of commitment failure. Weak public market information, the lack of grain standardization, the oral nature of contracts, and limited legal enforcement of contracts are all factors that contribute to the difficulty that traders encounter in attempting to trade directly with unknown partners. Using primary data, this chapter demonstrates that brokers enable traders to circumvent commitment failure and facilitate anonymous trade. Analysis reveals that brokers perform multiple functions in the grain market, among which are acting as inspectors and witnesses to each transaction and guaranteeing that contracts will be enforced, supporting impersonalized exchange in the Ethiopian grain market. In addition, brokers deliver "public goods," such as market information and product classification, as well as playing a key role in price discovery. Brokers thus determine market-clearing prices of a large number of grains according to very specific attributes of type and quality, enabling highly differentiated products to be traded in a systematic fashion. In terms of market volume, brokers handle roughly half of transactions by wholesalers and 16 percent of the total marketed surplus of grain.

CHAPTER 5

Rules and Norms Underlying Relations between Traders and Brokers

With brokers acting on behalf of traders, the relationship between them is essentially that of principal and agent. Like most principal-agent relationships, the trader-broker relationship is characterized by information asymmetry, because traders have relatively less information on market prices and equally little information on the actual behavior of their brokers. This information asymmetry, exacerbated by the physical distance separating regional wholesalers and brokers, gives rise to moral hazard and opportunism on the part of brokers. In order for the institution of brokerage to be sustained and to be more efficient than the alternatives, there must be norms to provide incentives for brokers not to cheat their clients, the traders. Norms can be viewed as voluntary conventions that facilitate contract enforcement (Aoki 1998).

This chapter, using primary data from trader and broker surveys, closely examines several aspects of the principal-agent relationship between traders and brokers, defined as their agency relations. Elements of trader-broker agency relations include the basis of the relationship, the extent of traders' dependence on brokers, the transparency of brokers' operations to traders, and the extent to which conflict is manifest in the relations. The chapter begins by systematically analyzing the norms embedded in the brokerage institution that limit moral hazard and sustain the function of brokers.

The Basis of Agency Relations

Relations between traders and brokers appear to be based on repeated interaction and exclusive relations. Thus, 87 percent of brokers' transactions are with long-term clients (Table 5.1). On average, traders have worked with the same brokers for six years (Table 5.2).[17] Moreover, 59 percent of traders appear to work exclusively with a single broker. There is significant variation in the exclusivity of traders' relations with brokers, with 74 percent to 100 percent of traders in surplus regions engaged in exclusive relations compared with 22 percent of traders in the central market.

[17] Similarly, Fafchamps (1996b) finds an average of 4.1 years of business relations among firms in Ghana.

Table 5.1 Brokers' relations with trader clients, 1996

	Percentage of brokers	N
Basis of broker-trader relations		
Referral	50.0	17
Common region	42.9	17
Anonymous meeting	7.1	17
Flat fee payment	92.9	17
When no partner is found for client		
Broker charges client for storage	71.4	17
Broker rents outside space for client	7.1	17
Broker buys/sells grain at market price	7.1	17
Broker stores grain without charge	14.3	17
If partners meet, future direct exchange is likely	21.4	17

	Mean	Coefficient of variation	N
Percentage of transactions with long-term clients	87.43	0.16	17
Percent transactions with distant buyer clients from same region	16.00	2.19	17
Percent transactions with distant seller clients from same region	17.89	1.95	17
Percent transactions where broker			
Represents both buyer and seller	7.36	3.62	17
Represents buyer only	16.21	0.57	17
Represents seller only	76.43	2.11	17
Percent transactions with			
Immediate matching of partners	77.53	0.14	17
No match—rent storage to client	17.00	0.63	17
No match—buy or sell on own account	6.68	1.65	17
Percent transactions with			
Only buyer present	37.36	0.63	17
Only seller present	3.73	3.63	17
Both buyer and seller present	53.68	0.49	17
Neither buyer nor seller present	0.77	2.44	17

Source: Author's survey, 1996.

A particular feature of trader-broker relations is that not only do traders work exclusively with a broker, but traders in a given location all tend to work with the same broker.[18] Thus, brokers obtain 50 percent of their clients through traders' referrals and 43 percent from having other clients in the same region (Table 5.1).

It is generally uncommon for a broker to represent both a buyer and a seller in a given transaction, with only 7 percent of brokers' transactions falling into this category. Similarly, it is relatively rare for brokers to trade on their own account with their own clients. That is, if the brokers surveyed did not find a partner for a client, only 7 percent engaged in transactions that involved directly buying grain from or selling grain to the client (Table 5.1).

Due to the sensitivity of respondents to ethnicity-oriented questions, the issue of ethnic origin was addressed by asking about the region of origin, or birthplace, which is culturally interpreted as one's ethnic roots. However, responses can be biased in that several ethnic groups may coexist in certain regions, though not all. The results suggest that ethnicity does not appear to be a significant basis for agency relations in that, while the proportion of traders with the same ethnic

[18] Thus, each broker in Addis Ababa is specialized in handling transactions from a particular set of markets in a region. Brokers who handle grain from the same area have their stalls adjacent to each other, enabling the rapid transmission of price and market information.

Table 5.2 Traders' relations with brokers, 1996

	Percentage of traders	N
Percent traders using brokers regularly	85.5	152
Percent traders not able to operate without broker	33.8	152
Percent traders working exclusively with a single broker	59.2	152
Percent traders with kinship ties with broker	3.9	152
Percent traders from same region as broker	26.5	152

	Mean	Coefficient of variation	N
Years of exclusive relations with broker	5.6	1.17	152
Percent transactions where broker gives sales advance or buyer credit	68.21	0.55	152
Percent local transactions where trader is present with broker	82.42	0.42	152
Percent distant transactions where trader is present with broker	43.88	0.95	152

Source: Author's survey, 1996.

origin as their brokers ranged from 8 percent to 54 percent between regions, only 26 percent of all traders were from the same regions as their brokers. As further confirmation, only 4 percent of traders revealed that they had "kinship" ties with their brokers (Table 5.2).

Similarly, brokers reported that, on average, only 16 percent of distant buyer clients and 18 percent of distant seller clients were from the same region. The relative weakness of ethnicity as a basis of agency relations is a striking departure from other studies of trust-based trading networks, in which ethnicity plays a major role (Fafchamps 1992a, 1996b; Greif 1993; Evers and Schrader 1994).

Traders' Dependence on Brokers

The majority of Ethiopian grain traders (as reflected by 85 percent of the survey sample) use brokers regularly. The level of their dependence on brokerage, as measured by whether the traders perceived it was possible to carry out long-distance trade without brokers, varied across regions. On average, 34 percent of the sample perceived that they could not operate in the grain market without brokers (Table 5.2). A greater share of traders in surplus markets, ranging from 26 percent to 70 percent, felt they could not operate in distant markets without a broker, while all traders in the deficit regions (with the exception of Dessie and Kombolcha markets) and the central market considered it possible to trade without brokers. In general, regional buyers are more likely to travel the distance to the central market and purchase the grain themselves, while regional sellers are more likely to work closely with brokers by means of telephone transactions. This finding may have to do with the opportunity cost of time faced by regional sellers of grain, who are busy purchasing grain from smaller rural markets and whose business would suffer if they were obliged to travel to the central market for each long-distance sale.

Another significant feature of the trader-broker relationship is that traders receive some form of financial credit from their brokers. The traders surveyed received either a sales advance or a buyer credit for 68 percent of their transactions, suggesting that brokers play a more important role than search and enforcement (Table 5.2).

Openness of Trader-Broker Relations

The absence of a public market information system and the physical distance between regional traders and central market brokers in Ethiopia result in high monitoring costs for traders to monitor brokers' actions. Traders suspect that brokers occasionally "skim"

Table 5.3 Openness and conflict between brokers and traders, 1996

	Surplus ($N = 64$)	Deficit ($N = 51$)	Central ($N = 37$)	Total ($N = 152$)
Percentage of traders who cross-check information from broker	80.6	80.9	64.7	78.6
Percentage of traders to whom broker reveals identity of trading partner	53.5	74.4	66.7	63.7
Percentage of transactions in which traders know their trading partners	64.71 (38.01)	75.70 (38.78)	58.21 (30.10)	68.21 (37.65)
Percentage of traders who consider trading directly without broker	82.7	72.1	66.7	76.4
Percentage of traders who feel direct trading would cause conflict with broker	27.9	51.6	50.0	39.3
Percentage of traders who have experienced conflict with broker	33.9	31.1	42.1	34.1
Number of conflicts in past year with broker	1.78 (3.38)	0.88 (1.31)	2.07 (2.99)	1.47 (2.73)
Percentage of traders for whom conflict was resolved through legal recourse	0.0	12.5	0.0	4.3
Percentage of traders for whom conflict was resolved through mediation	63.6	50.0	100.0	65.2

Source: Author's survey, 1996.

additional profits off the actual prices they obtain in the market as opposed to the prices that they convey to the traders, a practice referred to as *ferque*. Thus, 79 percent of all traders generally attempt to cross-check information provided by their brokers (Table 5.3).

The extent to which brokers inform their clients about the identities of buyers or sellers whom they have discovered is a potential indicator of the openness of agency relations. Overall, 64 percent of traders are informed of their trading partners' identities, although there is very wide variation between regions (Table 5.3). With the exception of traders in the Dessie and Kombolcha markets, more traders in deficit regions were provided with this information. This is due to the considerably higher frequency of transactions at which buyers are physically present in the central market, 92 percent of brokers' transactions, compared to 58 percent for sellers.

A possible result of providing partner information to clients is that with this information traders would attempt to bypass their brokers and trade directly among themselves. Overall, 76 percent of traders indicated that they would consider direct exchange without their brokers. However, 39 percent of traders felt that the implication would be to enter into conflict with their broker, if they were to do so (Table 5.3). In contrast, relatively few brokers (21 percent) felt that direct exchange was likely to occur without their involvement as witnesses and facilitators of transactions (Table 5.1).

Conflict between Traders and Brokers

Conflict between traders and brokers may arise when traders suspect price misinformation by brokers or when traders attempt to bypass their brokers and exchange directly with partners whom their brokers found in previous transactions. Yet relatively few traders surveyed (34 percent) had ever experienced conflict with their brokers during the entire period of their working relations, and the average number of conflicts for a year (1.5) had a very high coefficient of variation (Table 5.3).

The majority of traders (65 percent of the sample) used informal mediation as a means of resolving conflicts, with the share of traders using this option ranging from 40 percent to 100 percent (Table 5.3). In sum, relations between traders and brokers appear to be characterized by relatively little conflict and the absence of legal recourse. The widespread use of informal mediation rather than legal recourse is consistent with the existence of generalized social norms that govern economic relations (Platteau 1994b).

Incentive-Compatible Norms Sustaining Agency Relations

The sustainability of the brokerage institution over time depends on the extent to which brokers are prevented from abusing the trust of their clients. Without institutional constraints limiting the possibility of opportunistic behavior by brokers, trader-broker relations would be characterized by a higher incidence of conflict and would not be self-enforcing. In the absence of any market regulation of their function and given the high costs of monitoring the activities of brokers, what norms prevail to limit cheating by brokers and maintain long-term agency relations between brokers and traders?

Effective Transmission of Information on Brokers' Reputations

Agency relations are structured in a manner that provides a means for sanctioning brokers' actions. Thus, the practice of many traders in the same market working exclusively with the same broker would appear to give brokers significant market power vis-à-vis the individual traders in a market. However, this practice actually offers a safety net for individual traders in that information provided by the brokers flows freely among all traders in a given market. This enables traders to monitor the reputations of brokers, because if a broker cheats one client, other traders are likely to find out about it and spread the news, compromising the cheating broker's relations with all clients in that market and in nearby markets of the region. Evidence suggests that traders actually do carry out sanctions and effectively boycott brokers. For example, over the course of the survey visits, traders in the Nekempte market collectively boycotted their broker and together switched to a new broker.

The Absence of "Market Making"

A second means of limiting opportunistic behavior by brokers lies in the incentive compatibility of brokers relative to their clients. A potential source of conflict in agency relations would exist if brokers, trading on their own account, bought and sold grain from their own clients.[19] As noted earlier, it is not common practice for grain brokers to buy or sell clients' grain on their own account, at least overtly, in the interests of maintaining neutrality vis-à-vis their client traders.[20] Thus, the grain market structure does not have a role for "market makers" who openly purchase unmatched orders at a discount (the bid price) and sell unmatched orders at a premium (the asking price) in order to create a market for those willing to pay the price of immediacy (Demsetz 1968).

The brokers surveyed reiterated that trading on their own account is considered a serious breach of the implicit rules governing agency relations. Because information on purchase and sale orders is incomplete at any given point in time, traders cannot confirm a broker's information that a partner is unavailable. Brokers would be willing to transact at rates more favorable than the market, thus causing strains in their relations with clients.[21]

[19] A number of commodity exchanges, such as the Chicago Board of Trade, prohibit house trading by brokers in order to limit "frontrunning," whereby brokers trade on their own account before placing clients' orders, of which they know in advance.

[20] Although brokers stated that they do not trade directly with their own clients, many are engaged in grain trade. Thus, brokers may conduct undetected "frontrunning," in which case they would be reluctant to reveal the identity of their partners.

[21] Matching remaining orders at the market price would not be economically rational behavior for a broker, who would incur market risk in the process.

Flat Commission Rates

Third, Ethiopian grain brokers are compensated for their services by means of a fixed commission that is a flat rate per quantity transacted rather than a percentage of the final transaction price. This practice is common to all regions of Ethiopia studied and was confirmed by 93 percent of the brokers surveyed (Table 5.1). Lirenso (1993) also noted this payment system in the Ethiopian grain market in 1992. The flat fee is fixed across brokers and across time, but varies according to region.[22]

The practice of charging fixed brokerage fees has also been noted in other studies, in rural Indian foodgrain markets by Lele (1971) and in northern Nigerian grain markets by Gilbert (1969). Historical records from the late 19th century indicate that brokerage fees for grain traded on the Chicago Board of Trade were flat fees per quantity and were fixed across time.[23] Flat fees are also found in other international commodity markets, such as those for coffee and cocoa. In these markets both sellers and buyers pay commission fees, as is the case in the Ethiopian grain market.

In the Ethiopian grain market, a flat brokerage fee is compatible with broker incentives for several reasons. First, brokers do not usually act as dual agents; they represent only one of the trading partners. Thus, they receive a commission from only one party in the transaction. In a given transaction, both the seller's agent and the buyer's agent receive commissions from their clients. Second, the service for which brokers are compensated is not price search, given that there is a spot price that prevails in the market, but rather the search for buyers or sellers. For this reason, brokers maximize profit across a large volume of transactions in a short period of time, charging a small transaction fee. Third, and most important in the Ethiopian market, a flat commission limits cheating by brokers. Since brokers themselves determine the market price in the price discovery role described earlier, a percentage fee would bias the price discovery process and provide brokers with incentives to fix the prices to their advantage.

Summary

A close investigation of the agency relations between traders and brokers highlighted the importance of long-term, reputation-based relations in a structure in which many traders in a given market work with the same brokers. Ethnicity does not seem to be an important factor in these relations. The analysis revealed that, although traders attempt to monitor their brokers' activities, relatively little conflict occurs. Conflict is avoided through established norms that limit brokers' opportunistic behavior and that are incentive-compatible for brokers. These norms include the joint client system that enables traders to share information regarding their common broker, the absence of market-making by brokers, and the flat fee system.

The implications of these findings for policy are that strengthening the role of brokers further promotes anonymous exchange. At present, although a large proportion of traders use brokers regularly, fewer than half of traders' total transactions are conducted using brokers. Despite the higher search capacity of brokers, less than 20 percent of the total annual marketable surplus is exchanged through brokers (Gebremeskel, Jayne, and Shaffer 1998). This implies that formalizing the brokerage function could have significant positive consequences for the Ethiopian grain economy.

[22] Brokers charge different fees for grain coming from different regions. The fee is the same for all brokers handling grain from the same region, and changes in the fee are jointly determined by the brokers.

[23] See Chicago Board of Trade (1888).

CHAPTER 6

Transaction Costs and Social Capital

Market search is costly, both in terms of labor costs for search activities and in terms of the time cost of holding inventory during the search. For every transaction, each trader incurs the cost of labor time invested in search. This cost is represented by the opportunity cost of the labor employed in search, which depends on the trader's ability to hire additional labor or to engage the help of family members in the search effort. Second, each trader ties up his or her working capital in the form of grain for the time required to search. This cost is represented by the opportunity cost of the working capital during search, which depends on the trader's access to formal and informal sources of capital. Finally, each trader's search effort is influenced by the number of trusted contacts that he or she has, that is, the trader's social capital.

Search Time

Market search includes both the search for market information and the search for a trading partner. Market search costs are a function of the opportunity cost of a trader's time, the time spent searching, and the amount of search labor.

Table 6.1 compares traders' own search time, in terms of number of days spent identifying partners, with brokers' search time. These data were obtained by asking traders to recall for their last transaction how much time it took either them or a broker to find a partner. Traders who did not use a broker searched for 1.5 days, which was less than the broker's search time of 2.7 days. Comparing the number of price offers obtained, traders who did not use a broker had an average of 2.3 price offers per transaction, which was roughly equal to the number of offers obtained by brokers (on behalf of traders), who had an average of 2.5 price offers. These results indicate that traders do not use brokers when their search costs, indicated by the number of price offers they can obtain in a given amount of time, are lower than or equal to a broker's costs.

The traders interviewed estimated their own direct costs of search (including the costs of travel and telecommunications) per quantity transacted and compared these costs to the brokerage fee. As expected, traders who used the services of a broker calculated that their own search costs would be nearly double the brokerage fee, with an average ratio of 1.7. Further, 60 percent of traders who used brokers indicated that their search time would be greater without a broker, while 48 percent of traders who did not use a broker estimated that the search

Table 6.1 Search time and search costs per transaction, 1996

		Search time (days)	Number of price offers	Self-search cost/ broker fee
Using broker	Mean	2.7	2.5	1.7
	SD	(3.4)	(1.7)	(1.8)
With trader self-search	Mean	1.5	2.3	
	SD	(9.2)	(1.8)	

Source: Author's survey, 1996.

time with a broker would be at least equal to the time they spent themselves, confirming that traders' choice of brokerage is based on their own search costs.

Search Labor

Several alternative measures of search labor were gathered in the survey. Search labor is measured by the number of persons employed by the trader to help in searching for buyers and sellers and the number of persons responsible for purchasing and selling activities. Table 6.2 reveals that many traders do not have other staff to conduct partner search and to handle transactions, implying that the opportunity cost of their labor time is very high. The sample average for the number of employees conducting partner searches, including the trader interviewed, was 1.7, and the sample average for the number of persons responsible for sales and purchases, including the trader, was 2.1.

Alternatively, traders' search labor is measured by the amount of time spent daily consulting with other traders to obtain market information, identifying and negotiating with potential partners, and carrying out transactions. Traders spent an average of 39 minutes daily in market information searches and consulted with 5.2 persons (Table 6.2). The traders indicated that they conducted 1.6 transactions weekly on average. As a measure of their time constraint, the traders interviewed identified the incremental transactions that would be possible with the addition of another responsible helper who could act on their behalf. The traders estimated that the incremental transactions resulting from

Table 6.2 Search labor by region, 1996

	Number of traders consulted daily		Minutes spent daily in information gathering		Number of employees engaged in search		Number of employees engaged in sales		Number of weekly transactions		Incremental sales with additional employee	
Region	Mean	SD	Mean	SD	Mean	SD	Mean	SD	Mean	SD	Mean	SD
Surplus												
Wollega	3.36	1.29	42.73	31.73	2.73	1.79	3.09	1.70	1.43	0.91	0.27	0.65
Arsi	4.54	3.04	44.50	32.01	1.73	1.01	2.09	0.94	1.86	1.61	0.45	0.82
Gojjam	4.83	2.78	49.33	49.74	1.67	0.80	2.13	0.73	1.17	1.25	0.36	0.88
Deficit												
Wollo	4.23	4.41	25.18	40.64	1.24	0.75	2.06	0.83	0.66	0.46	0.11	0.29
Tigray	3.25	2.56	39.54	30.93	1.33	0.78	1.67	0.65	0.60	0.36	0.00	0.19
Hararghe	3.12	3.71	18.00	9.02	2.06	0.90	1.71	0.47	0.41	0.25	0.00	0.00
Central												
Addis Ababa	4.90	3.54	43.41	42.82	1.73	1.89	2.10	0.88	3.41	4.63	2.35	9.05
Total	4.24	3.28	39.06	39.79	1.74	1.29	2.09	0.93	1.56	2.62	0.74	4.52

Source: Author's survey, 1996.

Table 6.3 Traders' sources and use of credit, 1996

Source of loan	Percentage of traders who received loans	Amount of loan (Eth. Birr)[a] Mean	SD
Bank	30.8	26,723	64,657
Savings association	37.5	2,595	12,163
Friends	73.8	21,778	66,377
Family	31.9	5,537	16,046
Suppliers	67.1	32,114	169,723
Total credit received	90.1	88,917	218,733
Available working capital		55,184	62,647

Source: Author's survey, 1996.

[a] Eth. Birr 6.35 = US$1 in 1996.

adding a helper would be 0.7 transactions, which would add 47 percent to current operations (Table 6.2).

Working Capital

The opportunity cost of capital is a measure of how costly it is for a trader to tie up working capital in grain stocks for the period of time required for a transaction to be completed. Traders' liquidity preferences depend on how difficult it is to obtain additional sources of working capital, that is, their access to credit.

Table 6.3 reveals that the use of credit was prevalent among the traders sampled; 90 percent of them used some type of credit in their operations. However, far fewer had access to formal credit; only 31 percent had used bank loans. Informal credit extended by friends and family was considerably more important; 74 percent of the traders had used this type of loan. Supplier credit, which involves reimbursement of suppliers after a lag of one or two weeks, was used by 67 percent of traders. Traders received, on average, total credit of Eth. Birr 88,917 (US$14,000) for the marketing year, while their average working capital was Eth. Birr 55,000 (US$8,500), indicating either that part of the credit was used toward fixed costs of grain trading or that the traders occasionally supplemented their average levels of working capital with credit from family, friends, and suppliers. Although traders' actual use of credit allows a comparison of the importance of capital across traders, it does not provide a measure of traders' liquidity preferences, in that the use of credit is endogenous to their trading activities. Alternatively, traders' potential access, rather than actual use, indicates how liquidity-constrained they may be.

Traders are constrained from receiving bank credit primarily by their lack of collateral assets (Table 6.4). This is confirmed by the low proportion of the traders surveyed

Table 6.4 Access to formal credit by region, 1996

Region	Percentage of traders who have applied for bank loan	Percentage of requested loan received Mean	SD	Percentage of traders who own car	Percentage of traders who own home
Surplus					
Wollega	27.3	56.96	38.01	0	63.6
Arsi	72.7	63.86	17.36	18.2	81.8
Gojjam	56.7	61.25	21.56	0	55.2
Deficit					
Wollo	29.4	78.89	22.86	17.6	88.2
Tigray	33.3	39.49	10.04	0	75
Hararghe	23.5	100.0	0.00	5.9	58.8
Central					
Addis Ababa	6.7	52.5	31.81	13.3	23.3
Total	33.6	65.25	24.64	7.9	57.5

Source: Author's survey, 1996.

Table 6.5 Traders' access to informal and supplier credit by region, 1996

Region	Friends or family willing to give credit		Friends or family that gave credit last year		Friends or family to whom trader gave credit		Suppliers willing to give credit		Suppliers who gave credit last year		Buyers to whom trader gave credit	
	Mean	SD	Mean	SD	Mean	SD	Mean	SD	Mean	SD	Mean	SD
Surplus												
Wollega	3.45	1.97	3.09	2.30	3.18	2.71	4.00	0.82	3.00	0.82	3.91	5.66
Arsi	5.36	3.83	3.18	1.89	6.36	4.37	31.00	32.00	14.53	16.37	5.10	2.47
Gojjam	4.45	2.78	2.38	1.52	2.83	2.24	5.30	5.33	4.38	5.16	5.87	5.32
Deficit												
Wollo	3.06	2.16	1.47	1.70	2.59	1.58	2.21	2.61	1.79	1.58	13.75	17.67
Tigray	5.00	3.77	4.75	3.60	3.92	3.80	4.00	3.32	3.86	3.58	3.60	4.06
Hararghe	3.53	4.50	0.35	0.86	0.71	1.69	5.13	4.08	4.13	4.46	6.94	6.23
Central												
Addis Ababa	4.10	3.09	1.77	1.72	2.13	2.37	8.36	6.94	3.82	5.36	7.60	6.53
Total	4.10	3.20	2.20	2.20	2.79	2.91	7.06	10.73	4.54	6.77	7.03	8.53

Source: Author's survey, 1996.

who owned a personal vehicle (8 percent) or a home (57 percent).

Traders have a pool of friends and family as well as suppliers whom they can draw on for short-term credit (Table 6.5). However, the traders surveyed indicated that they had received loans from only between one-half and two-thirds of their potential creditors in the past year. This is partly due to liquidity constraints faced by these creditors themselves.

Social Capital

Factors that enhance a trader's social capital are whether his or her parents were in the grain business in the past, whether family members are currently in the grain business, how many languages the trader speaks, how many regular partners the trader has, and how many people the trader consults regularly (Table 6.6). Traders have more distant market contacts that they consult regarding market trends than they have contacts in their local market. On average, the traders surveyed had contacts in 3.5 distant markets and regularly consulted with 8 traders in distant markets and with 5 traders locally. Ethnicity and kinship are not important determinants of social capital; the traders surveyed indicated that, on average, only 1.5 of their market contacts were from the same region compared to their total number of contacts, 13 persons. Similarly, the number of contacts who were also family members was, on average, 1, while the number of "friends" in grain trade was much higher, with an average of 6 contacts.

The number of "regular" clients that a trader has is an alternate measure of social capital (Table 6.6). Again, traders have more regular partners in distant markets than locally, which is explained by noting that local transactions are smaller than distant ones and involve retail quantities bought directly from farmers or sold directly to consumers. Traders' social capital can also be characterized by the types of relationships, or the amount of trust, that traders enjoy with their regular partners. That is, social capital is enhanced if a trader can sell or purchase solely on the basis of a telephone conversation and if he or she receives or provides supplier credit to partners. Traders have an average of 4 partners with whom they transact only by means of telephone orders, representing one-third of the mean number of distant partners. The number of partners with whom they have credit relations is significantly higher, with an average of 13 persons.

Table 6.6 Social capital of traders, 1996

Regions		Surplus			Deficit			Central	
		Wollega	Arsi	Gojjam	Wollo	Tigray	Hararghe	Addis Ababa	Total
Local trade contacts	Mean	3.91	7.27	6.13	3.29	3.92	2.53	4.50	4.59
	SD	5.63	8.70	3.71	2.28	2.35	3.14	3.41	4.32
Distant trade contacts	Mean	5.82	7.55	11.28	4.65	5.36	6.76	8.93	7.89
	SD	5.49	5.41	7.67	7.15	3.78	5.24	9.60	7.46
Distant markets with contacts	Mean	3.82	4.45	5.60	2.12	4.50	2.47	1.73	3.46
	SD	3.57	1.51	3.06	1.83	3.78	1.55	1.51	2.86
Contacts from same region	Mean	0.82	1.64	2.57	1.82	0.42	0.71	1.43	1.52
	SD	1.08	3.64	5.86	2.88	1.16	2.02	3.67	3.77
Family in grain trade	Mean	0.73	1.18	0.77	0.47	1.25	0.41	1.07	0.83
	SD	1.01	1.40	1.68	0.87	1.66	0.80	1.51	1.38
Friends in grain trade	Mean	8.00	8.73	11.97	4.00	4.50	0.40	3.93	6.17
	SD	7.21	14.28	12.11	4.11	4.06	1.06	4.02	8.74
Regular local partners	Mean	1.00	5.64	7.93	3.76	2.75	5.18	15.57	7.49
	SD	1.84	5.29	5.11	5.12	3.57	6.08	8.78	7.70
Regular distant partners	Mean	15.70	24.89	13.93	16.06	14.00	8.65	8.3	13.07
	SD	11.04	29.32	7.80	33.17	7.73	3.20	10.26	16.59
Partners with telephone orders only	Mean	2.33	3.00	3.68	13.30	2.40	0.0	3.92	4.34
	SD	1.87	3.26	6.59	30.68	1.89	0.0	4.31	11.51
Partners with supplier credit	Mean	5.78	22.09	8.93	16.73	4.52		15.21	12.57
	SD	6.85	26.85	6.99	22.21	3.16		11.45	14.60

Number of distant markets in which have contacts (SD)	3.46 (2.86)
Number of contacts from same region (SD)	1.52 (3.77)
Number of family members in grain trade (SD)	0.83 (1.38)

Source: Author's survey, 1996.

Estimation of the Transaction Costs of Market Search

Each trader faces a unique set of transaction costs related to his or her costs of finding a buyer or seller with whom to exchange. The trader invests labor time in the search process and, because search is time-consuming, bears the opportunity cost of the labor time spent in search. Second, the trader bears the opportunity cost of tying up his or her working capital in the form of grain stocks while the search is under way.

Using directly observed search labor and working capital to explain traders' use of brokerage would result in endogeneity bias since the actual levels of search labor and working capital chosen by traders are not independent of their choice of brokerage. In order to avoid this bias, the opportunity costs of the traders' search time and working capital are derived as shadow costs from each trader's profit function. After controlling for physical marketing costs, such as transport, handling, and storage, each trader maximizes revenue subject to his or her costs of the labor time invested in search and the opportunity cost of holding grain inventory during the search period. Each trader is endowed with a unique distribution of trading contacts that directly influences his or her ability to find a trading partner. This distribution, or network, is considered a parameter of the trader's social capital and acts as a positive shifter in the trader's revenue function. The trader's revenue maximization is expressed by

$$\mathcal{L} = \gamma^{\delta} L^{\alpha} K^{\beta} e^{\varepsilon} - \omega L - \nu K, \qquad (1)$$

where

R is net revenue (revenue minus physical marketing costs),
γ is social capital,
ω is the opportunity cost of search labor (L),
and ν is the opportunity cost of working capital (K).

Table 6.7 Correlation coefficients for instruments for search labor and working capital

Instruments	Dependent variables		Instrumented variables	
	Net revenue	Value of sales	Search labor	Working capital
Number of languages spoken	–0.0029	0.0844	0.0969*	0.1129
Engaged in other business	0.0006	–0.0035	0.1294*	0.0416
Have others to manage business	0.0496	0.0951	0.6213*	0.0550
Age	–0.0828	–0.0592	–0.0897*	0.0445
Own home	–0.0915	–0.0691	0.0971	0.0428*
Have access to informal credit	0.0945	0.0753	0.1525*	0.2870*
Able to obtain bank loan	0.0709	0.0161	0.1334*	0.1940*

Source: Author's calculations, 2001.

* = Significant at the 5 percent level.

From the first-order conditions for profit maximization, the shadow opportunity costs of search labor, ω^*, and of working capital, ν^*, are derived as

$$\omega^* = \frac{\alpha R}{L} \tag{2}$$

$$\nu^* = \frac{\beta R}{K}. \tag{3}$$

Ordinary least-squares estimation of the traders' revenue function would result in asymptotically biased estimators because of the simultaneity bias that exists because both search labor and working capital depend on revenue and thus will not be independent of the model's error term.[24] To overcome this bias, two-stage least-squares estimation is used to obtain the coefficients necessary for deriving ω^* and ν^*. A rich set of instruments for search labor and working capital are obtained from the data, chosen on the basis of their impact on search labor and working capital without directly influencing revenue. The instruments used for search labor are access to additional persons to help with search, the number of languages spoken by the trader, the trader's age, and whether the trader has another business. The instruments for working capital are access to a bank loan, access to credit from friends and family, and collateral assets such as a home. The criteria for the choice of instruments are that they should be correlated with the variables that are being instrumented and uncorrelated with the dependent variable.

As shown in Table 6.7, these conditions hold. The estimation uses two alternative specifications of trader revenue. Net revenue, the net margin (after accounting for physical marketing costs) multiplied by the quantity of sales, is used in the first estimation. The gross value of sales is used in the second estimation. Search labor is measured by the number of persons in the trading firm who are engaged in searching for buyers and sellers. Working capital is measured by the average amount of funds that the trader has at his or her disposal for the purpose of buying and marketing grain. Social capital is a measure of the trading network that is available to the trader and is measured by the number of persons in grain trade whom the trader knows personally. This definition includes both a quality element, that is, the type of relationship that the trader has with other traders, and a quantity element.

Table 6.8 presents descriptive statistics on the dependent and independent variables used in the instrumental variable estimation of trader revenue, which is used to derive the

[24] This issue generally plagues the estimation of production functions. A solution is to apply duality theory, but this solution fails to use all available information and is statistically inefficient (Mundlak 1996). In this case, the existence of a rich set of instruments provides a more convincing instrumental variables estimator.

Table 6.8 Variables used in estimation of transaction revenue

Variable	Description of variable	Mean	SD
Dependent			
(ln) REV	Net trading revenue (Eth. Birr/season)	8.96	1.51
(ln) VSALES	Gross value of sales (Eth. Birr/season)	7.16	1.29
Search labor			
(ln) SLABOR	Number of employees engaged in search	0.72	0.36
Instruments			
OTHRESP	= 1 if trader has access to additional search	0.71	0.45
NLANG	Number of languages spoken by trader	1.89	0.80
OTHBUS	= 1 if trader has another business	0.22	0.41
AGE	Age of trader	32.83	12.30
Working capital			
(ln) WORKAP	Average working capital (Eth. Birr)	10.41	1.08
Instruments			
POSSBANK	= 1 if trader can access a bank loan	0.77	0.44
ACCESS	Number of persons trader could ask for loan	4.10	3.20
HOME	= 1 if trader owns residence	0.57	0.49
Social capital			
(ln) SOCKAP	Number of trading contacts	2.26	0.83

Source: Author's calculations, 2001.

ln = Natural logarithm.

Table 6.9 Results of instrumental variables estimation of transaction revenue

Variable	Variable name	(1) Net trading revenue		(2) Gross value of sales	
		Coefficient	Standard error	Coefficient	Standard error
Intercept	ln CONS	1.87	3.82	1.99	3.38
Search labor	ln SLABOR	0.75	0.40**	0.64	0.36*
Working capital	ln WORKAP	0.56	0.39*	0.88	0.34***
Social capital	ln SOCKAPzz	0.34	0.13***	0.23	0.11**
Adjusted R^2		0.28		0.22	
N		174		178	
Wald test of homogeneity		0.13		0.18	

Source: Author's calculations, 2001.

* = Significant at the 10 percent level; ** = significant at the 5 percent level; *** = significant at the 1 percent level; ln = natural logarithm.

opportunity costs of labor and capital for individual traders. As shown in Table 6.9, search labor, working capital, and social capital have positive coefficients, as expected, and are significant in both model estimations. The Wald test of the assumption of homogeneity reveals that the null hypothesis that revenue is homogeneous of degree 1 in search labor and working capital holds at the 13 percent confidence level.[25] The α and β coefficients generated from the two-stage least-squares estimation are used to derive the shadow opportunity cost of labor (ω^*) and the shadow opportunity cost of capital (v^*) for each individual trader.

An important issue is whether the instrumental variable estimation is undertaken at the expense of a significant efficiency loss in estimation. The adjusted R^2 of the ordinary least-squares regression of search labor,

[25] Tests for functional form specification were carried out with alternative specifications, such as translog and CES.

working capital, and social capital is 0.34 and 0.27 for the net revenue and value of sales model specifications, respectively. Thus, the instrumental variable estimation only slightly raises the root mean squared error from 1.22 with ordinary least squares to 1.26 in the revenue model and from 1.12 to 1.18 in the sales model.

The distributions of the estimated opportunity costs of search labor (ω^*) and of working capital (v^*) across traders are shown in Figures 6.1 and 6.2. More than 80 percent of the traders surveyed had shadow daily wage rates of Eth. Birr 20 daily (equivalent to US$6.00 in 1996) and greater (Figure 6.1). The shadow wage of Eth. Birr 20 was seven times the national income per capita per day.[26] And the mean daily shadow wage of Eth. Birr 44 for the traders interviewed was fifteen times the national average. This suggests that traders are time constrained. Moreover, there are limited opportunities for the majority of traders to increase their revenue through alternative uses of their labor time. As shown in Figure 6.2, the opportunity cost of capital is normally distributed across the sample population, with an average annual interest rate of 15 percent, which is significantly higher than the official bank interest rate of 10 percent in 1996. The higher variability of shadow costs of capital suggests that capital constraints may be more binding in terms of traders' market behavior, with a greater number of traders likely to opt for opportunities to reduce these costs. In sum, the distribution of both types of transaction costs across traders demonstrates the heterogeneity of individual market actors and allows for test the impact of these costs on the use of the brokerage institution in the Ethiopian grain market, which is addressed later.

Figure 6.1 Opportunity costs of search labor across trader sample, 1996

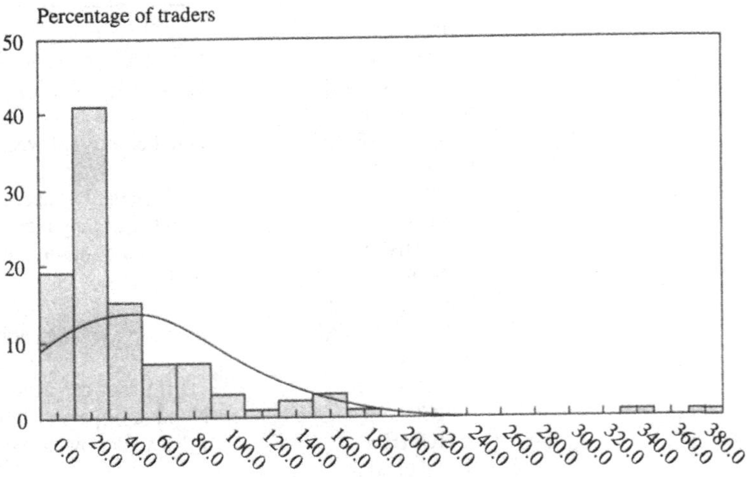

Source: Author's calculations, 2001.
Notes: Figure shows shadow daily wage (daily wage of incremental search labor). Eth. Birr 6.35 = US$1 in 1996. SD = 59.31; mean = 43.9; N = 101.00.

Figure 6.2 Opportunity costs of working capital across trader sample, 1996

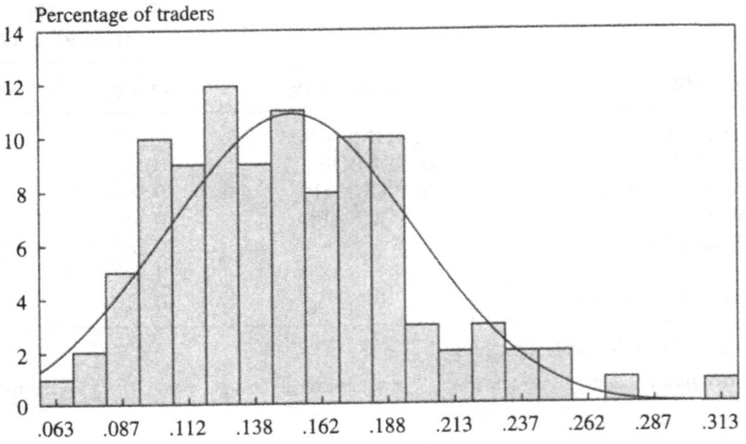

Source: Author's calculations, 2001.
Notes: Figure shows shadow annual interest (annualized interest rate over the study period). SD = .05; mean = .151; N = 101.00.

Transaction Costs versus Physical Marketing Costs

How important are these transaction costs of search relative to the physical marketing costs incurred by traders? There is an inherent difficulty in comparing these costs, because physical marketing costs are incurred relative to individual transactions, while the shadow search labor wage rates and the shadow interest rates for working capital are

[26] The average annual per capita income in Ethiopia was US$110.00, or Eth. Birr 700.00, in 1996.

Table 6.10 Annualized transaction costs and physical transfer costs, 1996 (Eth. Birr)[a]

Markets		Search labor cost	Percentage search cost[b]	Capital holding cost	Percentage capital cost	Marketing cost	Percentage marketing cost
Surplus							
Nekempte	Mean	7,803	7	4,925	5	102,128	89
	SD	12,807	5	7,402	3	103,310	8
Jaji	Mean	2,354	2	2,268	2	125,592	96
	SD	2,823	0	2,374	1	158,477	1
Assela	Mean	5,277	4	3,818	2	219,609	94
	SD	6,238	4	5,673	3	280,164	7
Sagure	Mean	863	2	543	1	34,190	96
	SD	1,197	3	684	2	13,595	5
Bahir Dar	Mean	5,727	12	4,834	7	72,414	81
	SD	9,884	19	10,460	11	112,788	30
Bure	Mean	3,691	10	2,149	8	77,475	81
	SD	5,202	19	3,086	17	74,228	36
Subtotal	Mean	5,078	9	3,836	6	97,786	86
	SD	8,521	15	7,790	10	142,267	25
	N	45	45	45	45	45	45
Deficit							
Dessie	Mean	1,447	5	979	4	41,453	91
	SD	748	3	641	3	35,301	6
Kombolcha	Mean	1,160	12	736	7	61,036	81
	SD	1,346	12	789	7	116,622	19
Mekele	Mean	1,842	6	1,052	4	38,358	90
	SD	2,857	8	1,701	5	21,983	12
Dire Dawa	Mean	705	17	369	8	7,819	75
	SD	475	11	313	6	11,629	17
Harar	Mean	3,282	24	1,530	11	30,457	65
	SD	3,233	26	1,299	11	62,888	36
Subtotal	Mean	1,866	14	996	7	34,310	79
	SD	2,342	17	1,124	8	58,420	24
	N	31	31	31	31	31	31
Central							
Addis Ababa	Mean	9230	17	5,730	11	262,269	72
	SD	14242	17	8,391	11	514,264	28
	N	19	19	19	19	19	19
Total	Mean	4860	12	3,288	7	109,970	81
	SD	9023	16	6,736	10	260,486	26
	N	95	95	95	95	95	95

Source: Author's survey, 1996.

[a] Eth. Birr 6.35 = US$1 in 1996.

[b] Share of sum of search labor, capital holding, and marketing costs.

estimated as either daily or annual rates. In order to compare transaction costs and marketing costs during the study year, both the estimated transaction costs and the per-transaction marketing costs were annualized. For search labor costs, the daily shadow rate was multiplied by the total number of search days per year, computed from survey data. Capital holding costs were annualized by adjusting the annual shadow interest rate for the number of days spent searching and multiplying by the working capital of each trading firm. Marketing costs were annualized by adjusting the annual sales revenue by the proportion of marketing costs. Although these calculations resulted in rough approximations and are subject to measurement error, they provide an idea of the magnitudes of different types of costs and point to interesting differences between types of traders.

As seen in Table 6.10, transaction costs of search represent an important share of the overall set of costs, representing 19 percent for the sample as a whole. The relative importance of transaction costs varies between types of markets. Transaction costs in the surplus markets represent 15 percent of total costs, compared to 21 percent and 28 percent in the deficit and central markets. This is partly due to higher overall marketing costs in the surplus markets. This finding suggests that traders in the deficit markets, who are engaged in long-distance purchases, face higher transaction costs than do traders in the other markets. Transaction costs appear higher for markets located in the Gojam zone and in Dire Dawa and Harar. Comparing labor and capital holding costs, transaction costs related to search labor costs appear higher for all markets. The next chapter explores the links between these transaction costs and traders' use of brokerage.

Summary

Transaction costs matter. The results of the survey of traders' search time and access to working capital indicate that traders are constrained in terms of both search labor and capital. Traders spend between one and three days searching for potential buyers or sellers with whom to complete transactions. Many traders do not have other staff to conduct searches on their behalf, suggesting that the opportunity cost of their labor time is very high. Further indication of this is that traders estimate that, at the margin, an additional staff member would increase their operations by 47 percent. In terms of access to capital, few of the traders surveyed received formal bank loans, mainly due to the lack of collateral. Traders that did apply for credit received, on average, 65 percent of the amounts for which they had applied. In general, 90 percent of the traders received some form of credit, whether from friends and family or other traders or in the form of supplier credit.

The survey also highlighted the importance of social capital in enabling traders to find trading partners more readily. The results suggest that, although traders invest in contacts in distant markets as well as in regular trading partners, ethnicity and kinship are not obvious contributors to social capital; fewer than one-third of trading networks are based on traders' common ethnic identity. This finding raises the possibility that some factor other than ethnicity may be a stronger determinant of traders' social capital.

In order to avoid endogeneity bias, the trader-specific transaction costs of search labor time and of holding working capital during search were estimated as shadow costs from the traders' profit functions. Instrumental variable estimation is used to avoid simultaneity bias, relying on instruments for labor and capital, such as languages spoken, other business, collateral, and access to credit. The results of this estimation of transaction costs reveal considerable heterogeneity among traders. They also suggest that traders may be more capital constrained than time constrained.

Comparing the annualized transaction costs of search with the physical marketing costs reveals that transaction costs are a significant share of the total costs. For the sample as a whole, transaction costs represented 19 percent of total costs. However, considerable divergence can be seen between surplus and deficit markets, with transaction costs playing a larger role in the deficit markets. This finding suggests that transaction costs might play a more significant role in traders' decision to use brokers for distant purchases. The following chapter examines this topic rigorously.

CHAPTER 7

Traders' Use of Brokers to Reduce Transaction Costs

Individual efforts to minimize transaction costs lead to the emergence of alternative institutional arrangements. The link between transaction costs and the emergence of institutions has long been recognized in institutional economics theory (Alchian and Demsetz 1972; Coase 1937; Hoff and Stiglitz 1990; North 1990; Williamson 1985). However, the inherent difficulty of measuring transaction costs at the level of market agents has limited empirical studies of whether particular institutions indeed effectively minimize transaction costs. Yet empirical analysis is particularly warranted in contexts in which agents operate in a weak market environment and transaction costs related to market coordination are very high, such as in the recently liberalized agricultural markets of sub-Saharan Africa and other economies in transition.

This chapter empirically tests the hypothesis that market agents are individually rational in using the services of brokers to minimize the transaction costs of search. The study of the brokerage institution in Ethiopia is particularly interesting because grain wholesalers are not obligated to use brokers for any or all of their transactions, enabling an empirical test of the determinants of their choice to use brokers. Thus, although 85 percent of the traders sampled in Ethiopia indicated that they used brokers regularly, they used brokers for only 30 percent of their total transactions, on average, suggesting that they chose whether to use brokers on a transaction-by-transaction basis. Despite the importance of brokerage in the Ethiopian grain market, a relatively large share of trade occurs in personalized direct exchange among traders who know each other well.

Traders' Use of Brokers

The choice of whether to use brokerage depends on the type of transaction, sale versus purchase, and the location of the trader, whether in a surplus or a deficit region. The traders interviewed in the 1996 survey who were located in surplus regions used brokers for 23 percent of all purchase transactions (Figure 7.1). In contrast, they used brokers for 49 percent of all sales transactions and for 66 percent of all distant sales transactions. The low incidence of brokerage use for purchases is due to the traders' practice of purchasing directly from farmers, while the higher share of brokerage use for distant sales is due to their practice of

Figure 7.1 Brokerage use by type of market and type of transaction, 1996

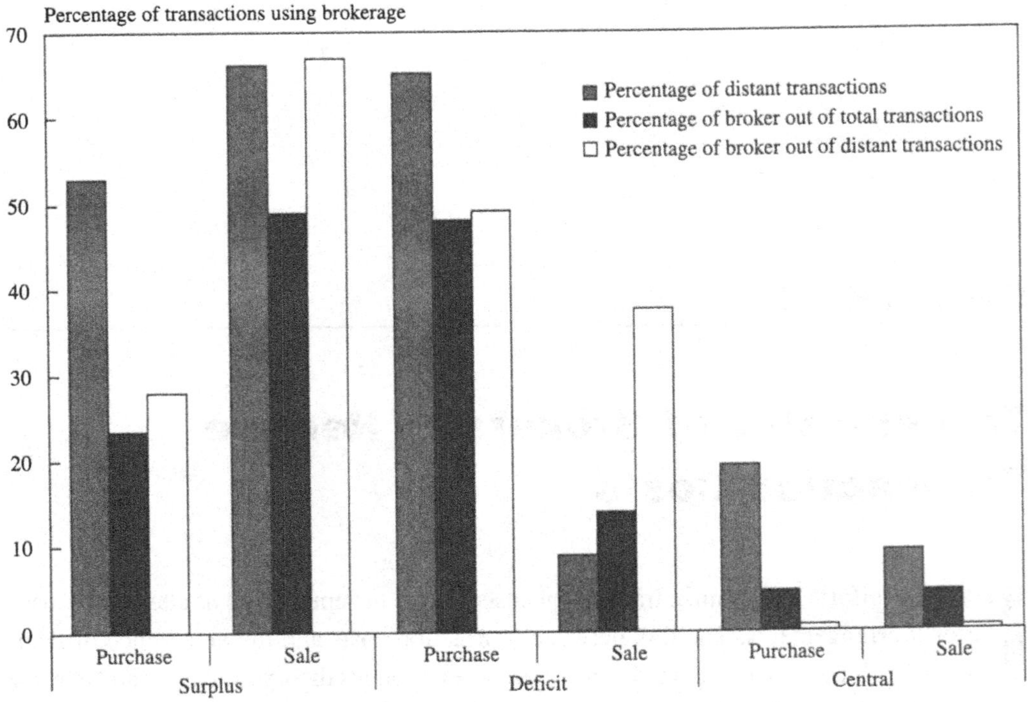

Source: Author's survey, 1996.

selling grain in the central market of Addis Ababa.[27]

Traders located in deficit zones used brokers for 48 percent of all purchases (Figure 7.1). The use of brokerage for sales by traders in deficit markets was significantly lower at 13 percent. This pattern reflects traders' practice of selling grain directly to local retailers as well as consumers. Due to their location, central market traders use brokerage only for local transactions, with use if brokerage for both sales and purchases of 4 percent, because central market traders tend to engage in transactions only locally. Wholesalers in the central market can buy directly from regional sellers who bring grain to the central market and can sell directly to local retailers, consumers, and millers.

For the sample of traders as a whole, without distinguishing by type of transaction, brokerage is used in roughly one-fourth of all transactions. Traders search on their own, either locally or in distant markets, in 72 percent of transactions. Thus, although the majority of traders (85 percent) use brokers regularly in their transactions, the proportion of brokered transactions among total transactions is relatively low compared to those accomplished by direct exchange. The coexistence of direct exchange and brokerage appears to be linked to the use of brokers for transactions in distant markets, sales for surplus market sellers and purchases for deficit market buyers.

The use of brokerage also varies across regions within a type of market and across traders within each of the regions. For pur-

27 The data used are self-reported figures provided by traders recalling transactions over six months. Given the low frequency of transactions, the recall period does not greatly increase error. Contractual choice data were gathered during two survey rounds. The results of the two rounds have been pooled, which provides a better estimation of the true values. Correlations between rounds are significant for data on the use of brokers and of self-search.

Figure 7.2 Use of brokerage for purchases by region, 1996

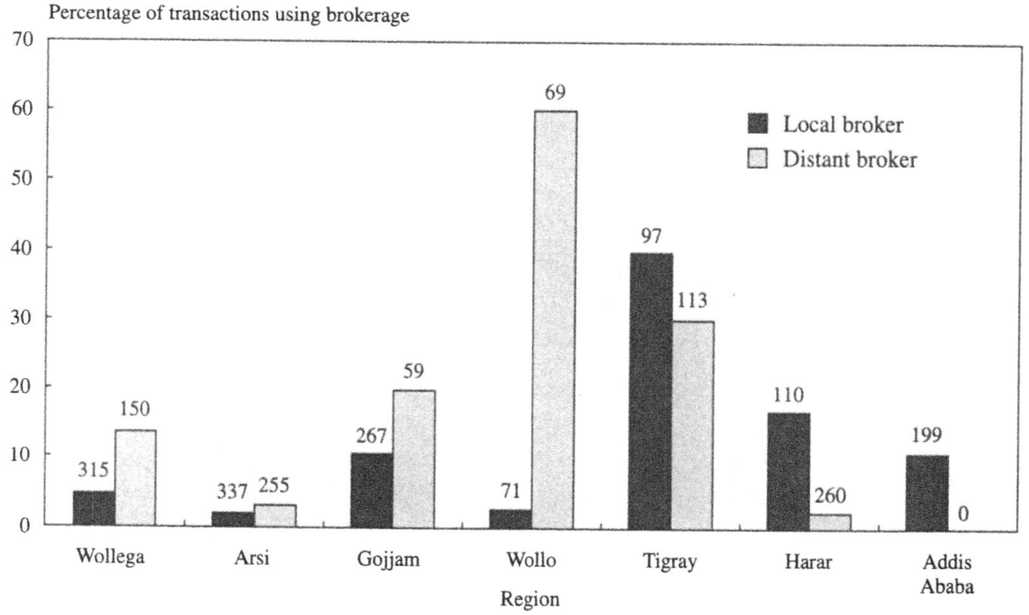

Source: Author's survey, 1996.
Note: Coefficients of variation are reported above the bars.

chases, there is a dramatic variation in the use of both local and distant brokers between regions within a type of market (Figure 7.2). Overall, the traders surveyed in the surplus regions, Wollega, Arsi, and Gojjam, used brokerage for a smaller percentage of transactions than did traders in the deficit regions of Wollo, Tigray, and Harar. However, within the deficit regions traders in Wollo and Tigray exhibited significantly higher use of distant brokerage than those in Harar, while the use of local brokerage is highly variable across regions in each type of market. In the case of sales, differences between regions within a type of market are less pronounced, with traders in surplus regions exhibiting high usage of distant brokerage compared to traders in deficit regions (Figure 7.3).

Heterogeneity among traders within each region is indicated by the coefficients of variation for the average percentages of transactions in which traders use brokerage for each region, as reported in Figures 7.2 and 7.3. The traders appear to have displayed significant variation in their use of brokerage for both purchases and sales, with at least 9 out of the 14 coefficients of variation exceeding 100 percent. In certain cases, extremely high coefficients of variation appear, notably for traders who used local brokers for purchases in the surplus regions and those who used distant brokers for sales in the Gojjam region. The heterogeneity viewed among traders indicates that factors other than the location, type of market, and even type of transaction influence the choice of using brokerage.

Long-Distance Trade and Brokerage

In constrained market environments, long-distance trade involves high coordination costs and considerable risk. Each trader is faced with the choice of either incurring higher search costs by trading in a distant market or trading locally, in a familiar market, where search costs are relatively low but opportunities are limited. In Ethiopia, grain wholesalers in regional market centers located 300 to 500 kilometers from the central market can either trade locally in their

Figure 7.3 Use of brokerage for sales by region, 1996

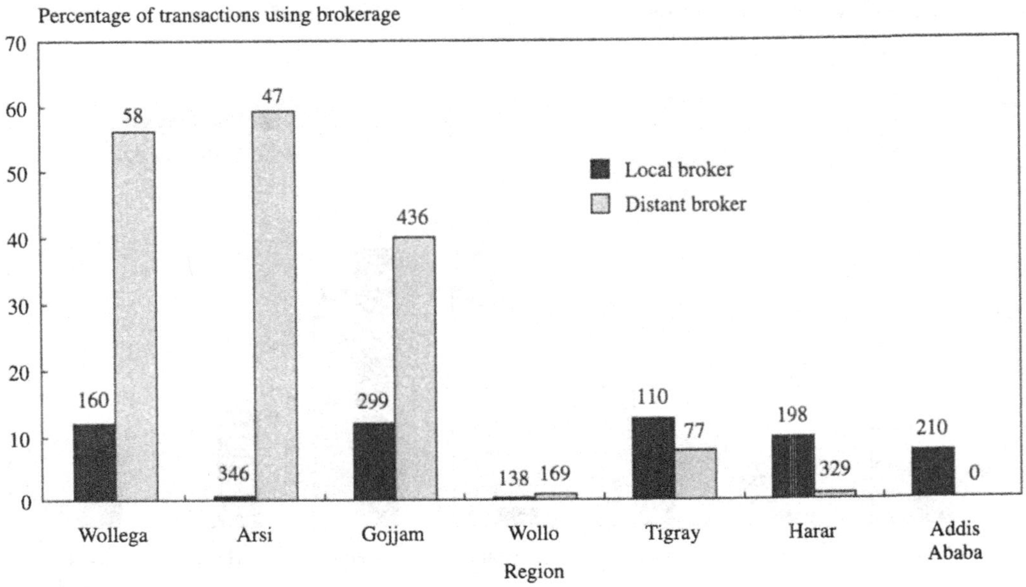

Source: Author's survey, 1996.
Note: Coefficients of variation are reported above the bars.

market towns or trade in the distant central market. This choice is partly determined by the type of region in which traders are based. Wholesalers located in surplus production regions tend to purchase grain locally from smaller traders and farmers and to sell this grain in the distant central market. Wholesalers located in the deficit regions tend to procure grain from the central market and to sell it locally to retailers and consumers.

Traders in both surplus and deficit regions have a relatively high proportion of distant purchases, 52 percent and 65 percent of total purchases, respectively, compared to central market traders, with 19 percent. Traders in surplus regions have a markedly higher proportion of distant sales, 65 percent, compared to traders in both deficit and central markets, with 8 percent of total sales (Table 7.1). As expected, traders located in surplus areas rely to a greater extent on brokers for their distant sales (66 percent) than for their distant purchases (27 percent). The converse is true for traders in deficit areas, with 48 percent of traders making distant purchases using brokers and 37 percent of those making distant sales using brokers. Central market traders do not use brokers for their distant transactions at all.

A Model of Traders' Sequential Choice of Brokerage

From the descriptive evidence it appears that each trader's use of brokerage is based on a two-tiered choice. First, traders decide where to trade, that is, locally or in a distant market. This decision is influenced by each trader's transaction costs, as well as by market-level effects such as whether other traders in the same market have a high proportion of long-distance trade. Second, traders choose whether to use a broker for each type of transaction (either sale or purchase) and for each location of trade (either the local market or a distant market). This choice depends on the percentage of the trader's transactions represented by long-distance trade, the trader's transaction costs, and regional effects, such as the location of the market in a given region.

Because long-distance transactions entail higher search costs and are enhanced by larger endowments of social capital than are

Table 7.1 Long-distance trade and use of brokers by type of market, 1996

Type of market		Share of distant purchases (percentage total purchases)	Share of distant sales (percentage total sales)	Share of distant brokered purchases (percentage total distant purchases)	Share of distant brokered sales (percentage total distant sales)
Surplus	Mean	52.06	65.49	27.49	66.18
	SD	36.53	34.50	36.63	37.69
	N	116	114	97	103
Deficit	Mean	64.73	8.25	48.45	37.22
	SD	41.02	15.71	44.53	47.68
	N	97	97	80	27
Central	Mean	18.57	8.58	0.00	0.00
	SD	35.14	22.44	0.00	0.00
	N	67	67	21	11
Total	Mean	48.44	31.80	33.04	55.47
	SD	41.63	38.51	40.95	42.98
	N	280	278	198	141

Source: Author's survey, 1996.

Note: These statistics were compiled from both rounds of survey data.

local transactions, the choice to trade in a distant market is endogenous to each trader's unique search costs and social capital. A percentage of a trader's total business that is composed of long-distance transactions depends on the opportunity costs of his or her search labor and working capital, as well as the trader's social capital and market-level effects, such as the trader's location. The average percentages of long-distance purchases (P_{-i}) and sales (S_{-i}) of other traders in the same market capture these effects. Thus, the percentage of a trader's total transactions that is devoted to long-distance trade is represented as

$$D_{i,t} = D(\omega_i^*, \nu_i^*, \gamma_i\, P_{-i,}\, S_{-i}), \qquad (1)$$

where ω_i^*, ν_i^*, and γ_i represent the opportunity cost of search labor, the opportunity cost of working capital, and social capital, respectively.

With the availability of brokers, traders who have chosen to trade at a distance in the central market face a second choice. Each trader compares the gains expected from searching directly without a broker with the gains expected from using a broker. A trader's net profit from searching directly is a function of the individual transaction costs of search, the trader's social capital, and the time the trader requires to find a buyer or seller in the distant market (τ). A general form for determining a trader's net profit from direct search is

$$\Pi_i^d = \Pi(\gamma_i, \omega_i, \nu_i, \tau_i). \qquad (2)$$

When a trader uses a broker, net profit no longer depends on the opportunity cost of search labor, the trader's social capital, or the time that he or she requires to find a buyer or seller. Instead, the trader's net profit from using a broker is a function of the broker's social capital (γ^b), the broker's commission (k), the opportunity cost of the trader's tying up working capital, and the time required for the broker rather than the trader to complete the search (τ^b). A general form for determining a trader's net profit from using a broker is

$$\Pi_i^b = \Pi(\gamma^b, k, \nu_i, \tau^b). \qquad (3)$$

A trader's participation constraint for using a broker is that his or her net gains are higher with a broker than with direct search, such that $\Pi_i^b \geq \Pi_i^d$. If the broker is more efficient in search than is the trader, $\gamma^b > \gamma_i$ and $\tau^b < \tau_i$. In this case, the difference between profits derived from using a broker and those derived from searching directly, $\Pi_i^b - \Pi_i^d$, is reflected in increases in the opportunity costs of the trader's search labor and working capital and in decreases in social capital. Because search costs are higher for long-distance transactions than for local ones, a trader's use of brokerage increases with the percentage of long-distance trade (Table 7.2). Thus, the percentage of the trader's total transactions that is devoted to brokered trade (B) depends on the transaction costs of the trader's own search, his or her social capital, regional effects (G), and the predicted share of long-distance trade ($\hat{D}$):

$$B_{i,t} = B[\omega_i^*, \nu_i^*, \gamma_i\, \Sigma\hat{D}_{i,t}\, (\omega_i^*, \nu_i^*, \gamma_i, P_{-i}\, S_{-I}), G]. \tag{4}$$

A recursive approach is used to represent participation in brokerage as a function of participation in long-distance trade, which itself is influenced by the transaction costs of search and by social capital. Recursive econometric models have been used to explain gift exchange (Ravallion and Dearden 1988) and technology adoption (Kumar 1994; Zeller et al. 1996). A two-step Tobit estimation avoids the inconsistent estimates of brokerage use due to the simultaneity bias that arises because trader-specific variables influence both the use of brokers and the share of long-distance trade.[28] In the first step, predicted shares of long-distance trade (D) are obtained from the Tobit estimation of (3). In the second step, predicted shares of long-distance trade ($\hat{D}$) are used to estimate the shares of brokerage use (B).[29] The use of censored regression rather than least squares is justified by the existence of a significant proportion of traders with zero shares of long-distance trade and of brokerage. Ordinary least squares would result in upward-biased estimators due to the selectivity bias that results from including only nonzero observations in the analysis (Greene 1993).

In terms of comparative static effects on the use of brokerage, the expected marginal effects of the opportunity costs of search and capital and of social capital on the use of brokers are obtained from the total derivatives of ω, ν, and γ with respect to B:

$$\frac{dB}{d\omega} = \frac{\partial B}{\partial \omega} + \left(\frac{\partial B}{\partial D} * \frac{\partial D}{\partial \omega}\right) \tag{5}$$

$$\frac{dB}{d\nu} = \frac{\partial B}{\partial \nu} + \left(\frac{\partial B}{\partial D} * \frac{\partial D}{\partial \nu}\right) \tag{6}$$

$$\frac{dB}{d\gamma} = \frac{\partial B}{\partial \gamma} + \left(\frac{\partial B}{\partial D} * \frac{\partial D}{\partial \gamma}\right). \tag{7}$$

The expected partial effects of higher transaction costs and long-distance trade on the use of brokerage are positive. Thus, $\partial B/\partial\omega > 0$, $\partial B/\partial\nu > 0$, and $\partial B/\partial D > 0$. However, the complete effect of transaction costs on B depends on the partial effect of costs on long-distance trade, $\partial D/\partial\omega$ and $\partial D/\partial\nu$. The expected partial effect of social capital on broker use is negative, $\partial B/\partial\gamma < 0$. Although the expected sign of $\partial B/\partial D$ is positive, the total effect of social capital on the use of brokerage is ambiguous, depending on $\partial D/\partial\gamma$.

Estimation Results for Traders' Long-Distance Trade (Step 1)

Tobit estimations of the share of each trader's long-distance trade are based on the shadow transaction costs obtained from both the net revenue and the gross value of sales instrumental variable estimations in Table 7.2. Shares of long-distance trade are estimated for purchases and sales separately in order to control for the effect of location on long-

28 A similar specification is used by Ravallion and Dearden (1988) to model transfer receipts and outlays, in which predicted consumption is used as a proxy for the regressand, posttransfer permanent income.

29 Using predicted rather than actual shares from the first Tobit estimation results in inconsistent standard errors. This can be corrected with a maximum likelihood estimation.

Table 7.2 Tobit estimation of the percentages of long-distance trade, 1996

		(Model 1) Net revenue				(Model 2) Value of sales			
		Distant purchases (percentage of total transactions)		Distant sales (percentage of total transactions)		Distant purchases (percentage of total transactions)		Distant sales (percentage of total transactions)	
Variable		**Coefficient standard error**	**Tobit elasticity**	**Coefficient standard error**	**Tobit elasticity**	**Coefficient standard error**	**Tobit elasticity**	**Coefficient standard error**	**Tobit elasticity**
Intercept	_cons	−293.91***		−419.04***		−255.54***		−365.76***	
		92.32		86.00		78.90		73.66	
Market share	$P_{j\neq i}$	0.72***	0.18	−0.45**	−0.18	1.50***	0.37	−0.36**	0.15
Distant purchases		0.11		0.21		0.20		0.18	
Market share	$S_{j\neq i}$	−0.22	−0.06	0.78***	0.32	−0.24	−0.06	1.93***	0.79
Distant sales		0.16		0.08		0.17		0.17	
Opportunity cost of labor	ln ω*	53.43***	13.36	75.02***	30.76	15.88***	4.00	26.13***	10.71
		19.60		18.04		5.76		5.32	
Opportunity cost of capital	ln ν*	48.99**	12.25	58.34	23.92	45.68**	11.42	54.03***	22.15
		22.01		20.13***		20.71		18.94	
Social capital	ln $\bar{Z}$	−23.91*	6.00	−41.73***	17.11	−3.40	−0.85	−15.02**	6.16
		14.69		13.58		7.61		7.06	
N		200		200		200		200	
SEE[a]		54.62		46.17		54.61		46.14	
Probability $(T > 0 \mid \bar{X})$									
Predicted		0.33		0.52		0.31		0.40	
Actual		0.25		0.41		0.25		0.41	

Source: Author's calculations, 2001.

[a] Estimated standard error of the regression.

* = Significant at the 10 percent level; ** = significant at the 5 percent level; *** = significant at the 1 percent level.

distance trading behavior, noted earlier. Unconditional or Tobit elasticities adjust the estimated coefficients by accounting for both the effect on the conditional mean of the dependent variable in the positive part of the distribution and the effect on the probability that the observation will fall in the positive part of the distribution (McDonald and Moffitt 1980).[30] Tobit elasticities are obtained by adjusting the coefficients by the Φ proportion of the sample that has nonzero observations of the dependent variable. In effect, this adjustment lowers the marginal effect by the probability that traders with no distant transactions would engage in some distant transactions as a result of marginal changes in the regressors.

In both model specifications, transaction costs have a large and significant positive effect on long-distance trade for both purchases and sales. Equations (5) and (6) suggest that the total effect on transaction costs on the use of brokerage will be unambiguously positive. Social capital also has a significant, though smaller, negative impact on distant trade, with the exception of distant purchases in the second set of estimations. Equation (7)

[30] McDonald and Moffitt (1980) suggest a breakdown of the slope vector into

$$\partial E[y_i|x_i]/\partial x_i = \text{Prob}[y_i^* > 0]\partial E[y_i^*|x_i, y_i^* > 0]/\partial x_i + E[y_i^*|x_i, y_i^* > 0]\partial \text{Prob}[y_i^* > 0]/\partial x_i.$$

The unconditional elasticity is obtained by scaling the parameters of the Tobit regression by the probability in the uncensored part of the distribution. See also Greene (1993) for examples and Ravallion and Dearden (1988) for an application of this method.

Table 7.3 Tobit estimation of the shares of broker use for distant trade

		(Model 1) Net revenue				(Model 2) Value of sales			
		Distant purchases (percentage of total transactions)		Distant sales (percentage of total transactions)		Distant purchases (percentage of total transactions)		Distant sales (percentage of total transactions)	
Variable		Coefficient standard error[a]	Tobit elasticity	Coefficient standard error[a]	Tobit elasticity	Coefficient standard error[a]	Tobit elasticity	Coefficient standard error[a]	Tobit elasticity
Intercept	_cons	−2187.29***		−1113.92*		−1914.33***		−966.14***	
		713.91		616.57		621.30		531.17	
Predicted	D_{purch}	0.70	0.22	−0.36	0.21	0.71*	0.23	−0.36	0.20
Distant purchases		0.53		0.60		0.56		0.55	
Predicted	D_{sale}	−5.84	−1.87	−1.37	−0.77	−5.87**	−1.90	−1.37	−0.76
Distant sales		1.80		1.20		1.90		1.09	
Opportunity cost of labor	$\ln \omega^*$	384.05***	122.90	205.83*	115.26	132.67***	42.45	61.43*	34.40
		148.76		120.38		51.97		38.14	
Opportunity cost of capital	$\ln v^*$	301.65***	96.53	188.06*	105.31	279.46***	89.43	175.31*	98.17
		127.31		107.40		124.64		100.09	
Social capital	$\ln \bar{Z}$	−231.82***	−74.18	−137.73**	−77.13	−94.50***	−30.24	−58.85**	−32.96
		85.91		74.44		35.34		30.87	
Wollega		438.53***	140.33	265.73***	148.81	484.60***	155.07	351.68***	196.94
		151.80		104.34		135.14		120.72	
Arsi		676.64***	216.52	256.55**	143.67	715.25***	228.88	366.89***	205.46
		224.41		113.47		191.95		143.74	
Tigray		108.79***	34.81	258.79***	144.92	104.74***	33.52	264.23**	147.97
		38.58		66.65		37.59		67.14	
Gojjam		421.90***	135.01	211.80***	118.61	506.61***	162.11	300.93***	168.52
		136.25		82.36		136.08		111.70	
Hararghe		−71.62***	−22.92	66.37	31.01	−64.59**	−20.67	65.97	36.94
		39.44		52.59		38.55		51.93	
N		151		116		151		116	
SEE		85.75		80.59		94.81		80.80	
Probability $(T > 0 \mid \bar{X})$									
Predicted		0.26		0.52		0.35		0.54	
Actual		0.32		0.56		0.32		0.56	

Source: Author's calculations, 2001.

[a] Standard errors are estimated from bootstrapping with 1,000 replications.
* = Significant at the 10 percent level; ** = significant at the 5 percent level; *** = significant at the 1 percent level.

implies that social capital will have an unambiguously negative effect on the use of brokerage. In contrast, market-level effects are relatively small, though highly significant and positive for the same type of transaction, either purchase or sale.

Estimation Results for Traders' Use of Brokers (Step 2)

In the second step, the share of brokered transactions is estimated using Tobit estimation for both model specifications, for purchases and sales separately (Table 7.3). In order to control for the effects of local use of brokers (that is, within regional market centers), the share of brokered transactions is restricted to brokers used for long-distance trade. The set of explanatory variables used includes regional dummy variables to capture the effects of regional effects. In a simultaneous system of Tobit equations, where predicted values of long-distance trade are used as regressors, standard errors of the estimated coefficients will be inconsistent. To correct for this, standard errors are estimated using bootstrapping with 1,000 replications, a procedure that provides generally very good estimates.[31]

The estimation results suggest that traders' use of brokers is individually rational in that higher transaction costs lead to increased use of brokers, while higher levels of social capital reduce the use of brokers, suggesting that the presence of brokers enables traders to minimize their transaction costs and trade more efficiently. In both model specifications, results are more robust for distant purchases than for sales. This may be because purchasing involves greater transaction costs than sales in that buyers must ensure that the quality and the quantity of the contracted grain will conform to their expectations and that delivery will occur in the appropriate time frame. In the net revenue specification (Model 1), the opportunity cost of labor spent in search has a larger effect than the opportunity cost of capital or social capital on the use of brokers. The high likelihood of receiving inferior grain or being quoted an incorrect price leads many traders to go directly to the central market to conduct purchases. Traveling to the central market, located up to 700 kilometers away, requires leaving a responsible manager at the trader's stall. Traders who are unable to do this and who are active traders have a very high opportunity cost of labor and are likely to use brokers for distant purchases. Transaction costs seem to matter less in the case of sales, perhaps because traders are not concerned with being cheated as to the quality of the grain. Typically, traders who ship grain to the central market must wait until sales are completed and they have received their payments before purchasing new stocks of grain. Highly impatient traders who seek to turn their capital around as quickly as possible are thus more likely to engage the services of a broker to minimize the time that their working capital is tied up in grain stocks. In the second specification (Model 2), the opportunity cost of capital has a larger effect on traders' use of brokers, although the magnitudes of the effects of both costs and of social capital are lower than in the first model.

Somewhat surprisingly, the predicted shares of long-distance trade do not appear to have a significant impact on the use of brokers, and their effects are minor relative to other explanatory variables even where these are significant, as for purchases in the second model. Finally, the region in which traders are located appears to have a very large and significant effect on their use of brokers, particularly in Wollega, Arsi, and Gojjam, the three surplus producer regions.

Summary

The transaction costs associated with searching for a trading partner vary significantly across traders, according to where traders operate, the types of transactions they are conducting, and their individual characteristics. A unique data set on Ethiopian grain traders' individual search efforts, access to capital, and trading networks, along with a rich set of instruments, enabled the analysis of the effects of these costs on trading arrangements made by individual traders.

An empirical model linking individual traders' transaction costs and their use of brokers was constructed to test whether traders were individually rational in choosing to use brokers in order to minimize the transaction costs of search. In testing this model, sample selectivity bias was avoided through the inclusion of traders who did not use brokerage. Simultaneity bias that would arise because the location of trade is linked to the use of brokerage was avoided by using predicted shares of distant transactions from a regression of distant shares against traders' transaction costs and social capital, as well as market-level effects.

[31] This procedure involves randomly drawing, with replacement, *N* observations from the data set and estimating the statistics for each replication. From the data set of estimated statistics one can estimate the standard error of the statistic. However, the point estimate used is the original observed statistic θ_{obs} rather than the average $\bar{\theta}^*$ from the replications (Mooney and Duval 1993).

The results reveal that, despite traders' heterogeneity, their individual behavior vis-à-vis the use of brokers is economically efficient. This finding suggests that traders operating in newly liberalized markets are "efficient but poor," to paraphrase Schultz's classic hypothesis, in that they operate within highly constrained, risky, and costly marketing environments. Thus, although traders exhibit optimizing behavior, they are nonetheless clearly acting in a second-best world. The results imply that the function of brokers is critical in reducing transaction costs and enhancing the performance of the Ethiopian grain market. In addressing the key question of how best to strengthen the performance of the private sector after market reform, this study supports the view that policymakers must have a clear understanding of the transaction costs faced by traders and their impact on traders' microeconomic behavior.

This study highlights that efforts to improve the overall efficiency of the Ethiopian grain market must be aimed at increasing the efficiency of the search function provided by brokers and at formalizing and strengthening their specialized role in the market, which will particularly benefit those traders with the highest transaction costs for search. The following chapter explores the effect of brokers on economic efficiency for the marketing system as a whole.

CHAPTER 8

Brokerage and Equilibrium Search Behavior

In most markets in which buyers and sellers are unknown to each other and search for a trading partner is time-consuming and costly, intermediaries such as market specialists, agents, or brokers facilitate the search.[32] The presence of intermediaries influences not only whether agents search, but also how much they search. In the Ethiopian grain market, how do brokers influence the intensity of traders' search? And what are the welfare effects of brokerage?

More search effort on the part of each individual trader leads to higher payoffs for all traders by increasing the probability that traders will meet. However, individual traders do not factor in the search effort of their partners when they choose the optimal amount of search effort that will maximize their returns from trade. This leads to a positive spillover, or externality, of each individual search that is not internalized into private decisionmaking about the amount of effort to put into search. Individually optimal search strategies diverge from those that would be chosen by a Benthamite "social planner," which would factor both partners' gains into the decisionmaking process. The presence of this externality in the decentralized economy results in a reduction of total welfare.

Traders differ in terms of how well they are able to search, that is, their search efficiency, and in terms of the opportunity costs of the labor and capital they invest in search. The presence of a broker in the search economy decreases the optimal intensities of search chosen by individual traders. The broker's greater search efficiency leads to increased gains from trade for both buyers and sellers among traders with less search efficiency, while traders with greater search efficiency may continue to search without the broker.

In a market with brokerage, traders who search on their own face a lower probability of matching with partners, because a subset of potential partners have gone to the broker. The presence of the broker in the economy implies that each trader's optimal choice of search intensity must factor in whether other traders have decided to use a broker or to search them-

[32] In labor markets, employment referral agencies fulfill this role; in housing markets, real estate agents; in financial markets, stockbrokers. I distinguish between two types of middlemen: "market makers" and "matchmakers." Market makers step in to buy or sell on their account when no partner can be found. They post a "bid" price and an "ask" price at which they are willing to sell or buy, at terms slightly more advantageous than the market price. Examples of market makers can be found on financial markets. In contrast, matchmakers only provide search services without entering the market themselves. Examples are real estate brokers and employment referral agencies.

selves, which partly internalizes the externality of search and leads to greater welfare. Thus, even when the broker is no more efficient in search than the average trader, the analysis shows that the presence of the broker enhances total welfare, because the gains made by traders with high search costs and low levels of search efficiency exceed the losses of traders with low search costs and high levels of search efficiency. The positive impact of brokers on economic welfare is not a general theoretical result, but is rather an empirical issue that depends on the distribution of search costs and search efficiency in the economy.

A Model of Bilateral Search

The conceptual framework used to analyze the optimal search behavior of traders builds on the search models of Rubinstein and Wolinsky (1987) and of Yavas (1992, 1994). Yavas (1994) saw the search intensity of traders as endogenous and based on differences in traders' price valuations. An important distinction from Yavas's model that is made here is that optimal search strategies are driven by differences in traders' search efficiency and costs of search rather than by differences in price valuations, because market prices are known with certainty and the real constraint is finding a suitable buyer or seller at the market price. Within a single period, all traders are assumed to be risk-neutral pricetakers.[33] When sellers and buyers meet, they trade at the competitive market price. Thus, differences in net profits per unit transacted are due to degree of search efficiency and search costs. Traders (sellers or buyers) face uncertainty regarding the outcomes of their searches. Thus, each trader has a probability Θ of meeting a partner, where $\Theta \in [0,1]$.

Each trader chooses his or her profit-maximizing level of search intensity, S for sellers and B for buyers, where $S,B \in [0,½]$. Each trader has an exogenously determined and unique parameter of search efficiency, $\gamma \in [0,1]$. For a given transaction, the probability of matching faced by each trader is a linear function of both the buyer's and the seller's search effort (S,B) and search efficiency (γ). A simple linear specification of the probability of matching that accounts for the differences in search efficiency between two trading partners is given by

$$\Theta(S,B) = \gamma_S S + \gamma_B B. \tag{1}$$

For a trader with search intensity S or B, the costs of search labor, C_L, and of holding capital fixed during search, C_K, are a function of search intensity (S or B), labor (L) and working capital (K), and the opportunity costs of search labor (ω), capital (ν), and search time (t) needed, such that

$$C_L(S) = S^2(\omega L t), \text{ and} \tag{2}$$

$$C_K(S) = S^2(\nu K t). \tag{3}$$

Search without Brokerage

A representative seller chooses S so as to maximize V_S:

$$\begin{aligned} &\max_S V_S(S,\gamma,\omega,\nu) \\ &\quad = \Theta(S,B)R_S - C_L(S) - C_K(S) \\ &\quad = (\gamma_S S + \gamma_B B)R_S - S^2(\omega L t) - S^2(\nu K t), \end{aligned} \tag{4}$$

where R_S and R_B represent the seller's and the buyer's net revenue from trading, respectively. Analogously, a representative buyer chooses B to maximize V_B: $\max_B V_B (B,\gamma,\omega,\nu)$.[34] The Bayesian-Nash equilibrium for the competitive economy is given by $[S^*(\cdot),B^*(\cdot)]$, such that

[33] In the Ethiopian market, there exists a competitive market price that is determined exogenously as a function of the daily supply and demand in the central market. Prices are determined in a quasi-bidding process by brokers before the market opens. Price discovery by brokers can be viewed as another externality of the presence of brokers that is not addressed here.

[34] From here on, to avoid repetition, mathematical expressions will be presented only for the seller, with the understanding that the buyer's functions are exactly analogous.

$$S^*(\cdot) \in \text{argmax } V_S[S,\gamma_s,\omega_s,\nu_s, B^*(\cdot)] \quad \forall\gamma_s,\omega_s,\nu_s, \text{ and} \tag{5a}$$

$$B^*(\cdot) \in \text{argmax } V_B[B,\gamma_b,\omega_b,\nu_b, S^*(\cdot)] \quad \forall\gamma_b,\omega_b,\nu_b. \tag{5b}$$

The optimal search intensity chosen by each type of trader is the level of search intensity that equates the marginal returns from search with the marginal costs of search. The optimal search intensities, S^* and B^*, are characterized by the solution to the first-order conditions of the competitive equilibrium. For the seller, these are

$$S^*(\gamma,\omega,\nu)\text{: } \gamma_S R_S = C_L'(S) + C_K'(S) = 2St(\omega L + \nu K). \tag{6}$$

Thus, S^* and B^* increase in search efficiency, γ, and decrease in the opportunity costs of search, ω and ν. This reflects what one might intuit, that traders with greater search efficiencies expect greater net profits from search and thus search more, while traders with greater opportunity costs of search expect fewer net gains from search and thus search less.

Externality Effects of Individual Search Behavior

Greater search intensity by either the seller or the buyer leads to a higher probability of finding a trading partner and to greater net profits for both traders. This gives rise to a positive externality of search behavior that is not captured because individual traders do not factor in the effects on their partners when making search intensity choices. Were there a Benthamite "social planner" who was concerned with the most efficient allocation of resources in the economy, the seller's and the buyer's net profits would be maximized jointly and the socially optimal choice of S^{**} and B^{**} would be based on the effects of this choice on both the seller's and the buyer's marginal revenues. In the socially optimal model, the choice of the seller's and the buyer's search intensities would be characterized as

$$S^{**}(\gamma,\omega,\nu)\text{: } \gamma_S(R_S + R_B) = C_L'(S) + C_K'(S) = 2St(\omega L + \nu K). \tag{7}$$

In a competitive equilibrium, with no "social planner," the allocation of search intensities is less than optimal, with $S^* < S^{**}$ and $B^* < B^{**}$.

Search with Brokerage

In the presence of a representative risk-neutral broker who does not trade on his or her own account, traders choose whether to use a broker and, if they opt to search on their own, the optimal level of search intensity. Each trader has a unique probability, μ, of using a broker in a given transaction. Since other traders in the market do not know this probability, each trader makes conjectures about the probability that others will choose the services of brokers. An important feature of this economy is that a trader who has opted to search without a broker can search for a trading partner among the pool of traders who are similarly searching on their own. Conversely, once a trader has chosen to use a broker, he or she exits from the direct search market. This phenomenon of dichotomization of the "direct search market" and the "brokered search market" is observed in the Ethiopian grain market, where traders who opt for brokerage physically ship grain to their brokers and stop searching on their own, while brokers who have received grain from clients tend to contact brokers who represent distant clients. This dichotomization can be viewed as the self-selection by traders into personalized versus anonymous exchange.

The choice of optimal search intensity depends on the size of the search market and on the search intensities of other traders. A trader i (either seller or buyer) who factors in the possibility that a possible partner j (either seller or buyer) will drop out of the search market and use a broker has the probability of matching of $\Theta_i'(S,B) = (1 - \mu_j)(\gamma_S S + \gamma_B B)$. When a trader uses a broker, his or her probability of matching depends on the broker's

Table 8.1 Optimal search intensities under four search models

Model	Sellers' optimal search intensity	Buyers' optimal search intensity
(1) Competitive model without broker	$S^* = \gamma_S R_S/2(\omega L + \nu K)$	$B^* = \gamma_B R_B/2(\omega L + \nu K)$
(2) Socially optimal model without broker	$S^{**} = \gamma_S(R_S + R_B)/2(\omega L + \nu K)$	$B^{**} = \gamma_B(R_S + R_B)/2(\omega L + \nu K)$
(3) Competitive model with broker	$S^{M*} = \gamma_S R_S(1 - \mu_B)/2(\omega L + \nu K)$	$B^{M*} = \gamma_B R_B(1 - \mu_S)/2(\omega L + \nu K)$
(4) Socially optimal model with broker	$S^{M**} = \gamma_S R_S(1 - \mu_B) + \gamma_S R_B(1 - k\mu S)/2(\omega L + \nu K)$	$B^{M**} = \gamma_B R_B(1 - \mu S) + \gamma_B R_S(1 - k\mu_B)/2(\omega L + \nu K)$

Source: Author's calculations, 2001.

Note: γ = Search efficiency; R = net revenue from trading; ω = opportunity cost of search labor; L = search labor; ν = opportunity cost of inventory capital; K = capital; μ = probability of brokerage use; k = brokerage fee.

search efficiency, γ_M, and search intensity, M, and is adjusted by the probability that the corresponding partner is using brokerage or not. Thus, for a seller,

$$\Theta_S^M(M,B) = (1 - \mu_B)(\gamma_M M + \gamma_B B). \quad (8)$$

The seller or buyer then maximizes W_S or W_B, the expected net profit with brokerage:

$$\max_S W_S = \mu_B(\gamma_M M + \gamma_B B)R_S(1 - k) - C_K^M(M) + (1 - \mu_B)(\gamma_S S + \gamma_B B)R_S - C_L(S) - C_K(S), \quad (9)$$

where

k is the brokerage fee,[35]

$C^M(M) = M^2(\nu K t')$ is the trader's cost of capital with brokerage, and

t' is the broker's search time.

Again, the optimal search intensity chosen by each type of trader is the level of search intensity that equates the marginal returns from search with the marginal costs of search. In the presence of the possibility of brokerage, the optimal search intensities, S^{M*} and $B^{M},*$ depend on the probability of the brokerage choices of other traders:

$$S^{M*}(\gamma,\omega,\nu)\colon (1 - \mu_B)\gamma_S R_S = C_L'(S) + C_K'(S). \quad (10)$$

Thus, brokers' presence introduces a strategic interaction term between the optimal search intensities of traders. Although search intensities still do not depend on the payoff from trade of a trader's partner, as is the case for the socially optimal model, traders' optimal search strategies depend on the proportion of traders who use brokers (μ), which partly internalizes the externality of individual search. The externality is only partially internalized, however, because the trader's choice does not depend on the partner's revenue, R, as in the socially optimal model.

In contrast, a search economy with brokerage and an "efficient" social planner would maximize the sum of the seller's and the buyer's net profits. The first-order condition that would optimize a seller's or a buyer's choice of search intensities can be expressed as

$$S^{M**}(\gamma,\omega,\nu)\colon (1 - \mu_B)\gamma_S R_S + (1 - k\mu_S)\gamma_S R_B = C_L'(S) + C_K'(S). \quad (11)$$

Traders factor in the possibility that the search market is reduced by the use of brokerage by their potential partners and also factor in the effects of their own choice of brokerage on their partners' net returns. It can be seen from Table 8.1 that, for $0 \leq \mu \leq 1$, $S^* \geq S^{M*}$ and $S^{**} \geq S^{M**}$. Under competitive equilibrium, the presence of brokers un-

[35] In the Ethiopian context, the brokerage fee is a flat fee per quantity (bag) transacted rather than a percentage of the sale price. Here the fee is represented as a proportion of transaction revenue, equal to quantity times price.

equivocally decreases the optimal search intensity. Likewise, socially optimal search intensities are greater than under competitive equilibrium both with and without brokerage, confirming that a positive externality still remains under brokerage. Finally, the relationship between search intensity in the socially optimal model with brokerage and in the socially optimal model without brokerage depends on the level of k, μ_B, and μ_S.

Application to the Ethiopian Grain Economy

The Data

Although every trader, by definition, buys and sells grain, the analysis distinguishes traders in surplus regions as "sellers" and traders in deficit regions as "buyers." For the purposes of this analysis, traders located in the central market are omitted, resulting in a sample of 47 sellers and 33 buyers. Data were obtained on each trader's search time, search labor, working capital, average net returns per transaction, trading contacts, and use of brokerage over six months. In order to calculate net profits (V_S and V_B) per trader in comparable units, traders' net returns (R) are expressed as returns per transaction, and costs per transaction of search labor and capital (C_L and C_K) are expressed as the product of the shadow costs per unit of labor and capital per day, the number of days of search, and the number of units of labor and capital. Since the actual levels of search labor and working capital chosen by traders are not independent of their choice of brokerage, the opportunity costs of the traders' search labor and working capital are derived as shadow costs from each trader's profit function. The parameter of search efficiency, γ, is an index ranging from 0 to 1 that is constructed by dividing each trader's social capital, that is, the number of his or her trading contacts, by the maximum number of trading contacts available to an individual trader in the economy.

The Importance of Traders' Heterogeneity

In order to determine whether traders' heterogeneity is a factor in his or her search behavior, the analysis initially compares the search intensities and surpluses when traders are homogeneous with search intensities when they are heterogeneous with respect to search efficiency and search costs.

A baseline scenario of the competitive model without brokerage assumes that all traders are perfectly homogeneous, with identical cost profiles, revenues, and search efficiency. The optimal search intensity chosen by individual traders takes a parameter value bounded between 0 and 0.5. In the case of full homogeneity, all traders have a low optimal search intensity of 0.08. The sum of all traders' net profits per transaction (after subtracting the opportunity costs of search labor and working capital per transaction) is Eth. Birr 597, which represents 3 percent of the sum of traders' gross revenues per transaction.

A second scenario of competitive equilibrium without brokerage relaxes the assumption of perfect homogeneity by allowing trader-specific search costs and revenues, although traders remain homogeneous with respect to search efficiency. As in the baseline scenario, all traders have the same parameter of search efficiency, $\gamma = .24$.[36] The results of this scenario are that the optimal search intensities of traders increase from the baseline scenario, from .08 to .15 in the case of sellers while remaining .08 in the case of buyers, because traders with lower search costs significantly increase their search effort. Traders who increase their search effort obtain higher payoffs from search, raising the sum of net profits in the market by 40 percent, to Eth. Birr 834, or 4 percent of gross revenues.

In the third scenario, still in a competitive economy without brokerage, traders are completely heterogeneous with respect to all variables: search costs, search efficiency,

[36] Recall that the parameters of search efficiency are 0 and 1 and represent an index of traders' social capital, which is constructed by setting the γ of the trader with the highest number of contacts equal to 1.

and revenues. In this case relatively search-efficient traders invest more effort in search, while less efficient traders allocate fewer resources to search. The more efficient allocation of search effort results in a significant increase in economic surplus, with the sum of net profits increasing by 181 percent, to Eth. Birr 1,677 per transaction, or 8 percent of gross revenues. These results indicate that the assumption that traders are homogeneous in search efficiency and transaction costs leads to highly biased estimations of the optimal level of search intensity in the market. That is, traders with a lower level of search efficiency than the sample average (in this case, .24) will demonstrate a higher than optimal search intensity under the homogeneity assumption, and traders with higher efficiency than the sample average will search less. This misallocation of search effort is demonstrated in Figures 8.1 and 8.2, where it can be seen that many sellers (who are relatively more search efficient) search less with the assumption of homogeneity and many buyers search more with the assumption of homogeneity.

In contrast, a comparison of sellers' and buyers' net profits under competitive equilibrium with heterogeneity reveals that a lower level of search on the part of buyers results in a lower level of average returns to buyers (see Figure 8.3).

Individual versus Socially Optimal Search without Brokerage

Sharp differences in search intensities are apparent between the competitive equilibrium and the joint welfare model. As shown in Figures 8.4 and 8.5, the results confirm that in the presence of a positive externality, as noted earlier, individual search intensities are lower than the social optimum. In comparison with the competitive model with heterogeneous traders, the level of search intensity rises from .15 to .28 for sellers and from .08 to .28 for buyers.

Sellers' search behavior under competitive equilibrium appears to be closer to the socially desirable search intensity level than

Figure 8.1 Comparison of sellers' search intensities, homogeneous versus heterogeneous sellers, 1996

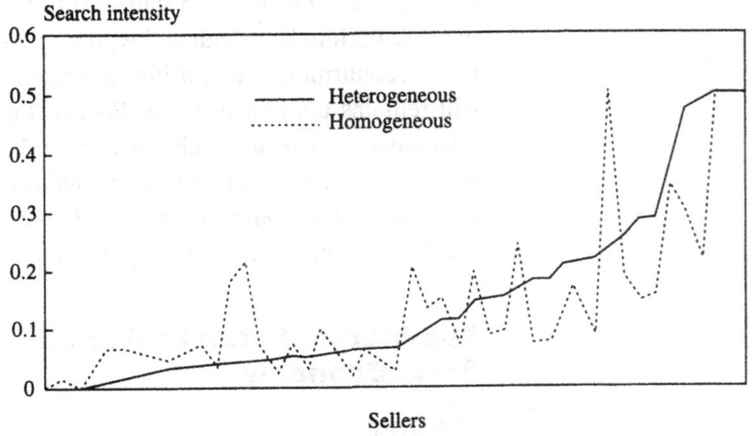

Source: Author's calculations, 2001.

is that of buyers. Under competitive conditions, buyers demonstrate very low search intensities, with an average search intensity parameter of .08, compared to the average search intensity of .15 for sellers. This result could be rooted in either differences in search costs between sellers and buyers or differences in search efficiency. In the sample data there are greater differences in search costs between sellers and buyers than there are in search efficiency. Buyers had an average labor cost of Eth. Birr 231 per transaction and an average capital cost of Eth. Birr 172 per transaction, compared to sellers' average

Figure 8.2 Comparison of buyers' search intensities, homogeneous versus heterogeneous buyers, 1996

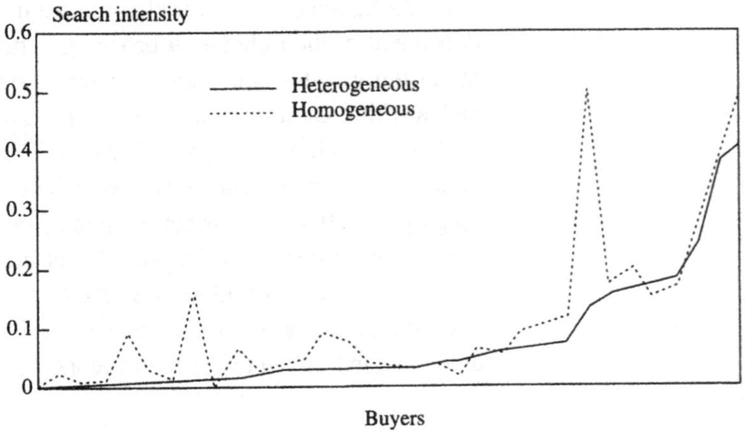

Source: Author's calculations, 2001.

Figure 8.3 Sellers' and buyers' surplus under competitive equilibrium, without brokerage, 1996

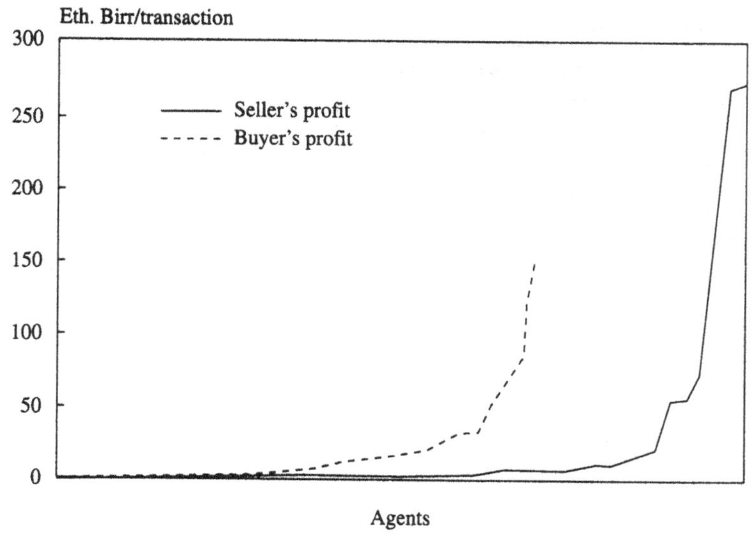

Source: Author's calculations, 2001.

search labor costs of Eth. Birr 207 and capital costs of Eth. Birr 154. These cost differences are explained in turn by the longer time needed to purchase grain rather than to sell grain, with an average of 3.6 days for buyers relative to 1.9 days for sellers.

Finally, in comparison with the competitive equilibrium model without brokerage, the sum of net profits in the joint welfare model without brokerage rises by 126 percent, to Eth. Birr 3,798 or 18 percent of gross revenues per transaction, due to the greater allocation of resources to search activities by all traders. This result demonstrates that socially efficient search behavior leads to positive welfare gains as the positive externality of search is fully internalized in the search allocation decisions of individual traders.

Figure 8.4 Sellers' search behavior, without brokerage, in competitive and joint welfare models, 1996

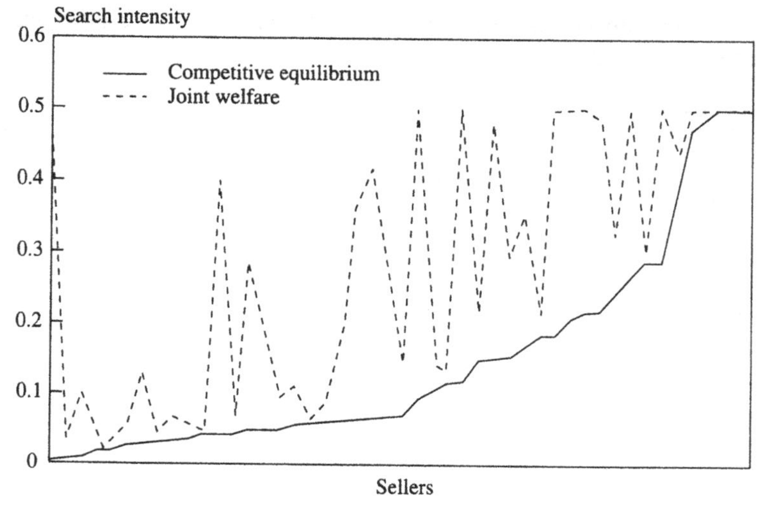

Source: Author's calculations, 2001.

Does Brokerage Internalize the Externality of Individual Search?

The profit maximization conditions of the competitive model with brokerage imply that the broker's presence enables traders to partially internalize the positive externality of searching for trading partners by factoring in other traders' decisions to use a broker. In other words, the positive spillover of better allocation of search effort from using a broker is captured in the market-determined brokerage fee. This premise is tested by separating the gains in welfare that are due solely to the broker's presence in the economy from those due to the broker's greater search efficiency. For this purpose, the case with homogeneous traders is extended to include a single broker with the same average search efficiency ($\gamma = .24$) as traders. In an economy with a broker who has the same search efficiency as the set of homogeneous traders, the sum of net profits across traders increases to Eth. Birr 959 per transaction. This is in comparison to Eth. Birr 834 in the earlier scenario of homogeneous traders without brokerage. This result demonstrates that even when the broker is not more efficient in search than the traders, there are allocative efficiency gains from having a broker in the economy.

The Effect of Brokerage on Heterogeneous Traders' Search Behavior

In the competitive model, the introduction of a broker into the search economy has the expected effect of significantly reducing traders' optimal search intensities. On average, sellers' search intensities decrease by one-third, from .15 to .10, and buyers' search intensities decrease by more than half, from .08 to .03. Figures 8.6 and 8.7 show that optimal search intensity declines considerably in every individual case.

Figure 8.5 Buyers' search behavior, without brokerage, in competitive and joint welfare models, 1996

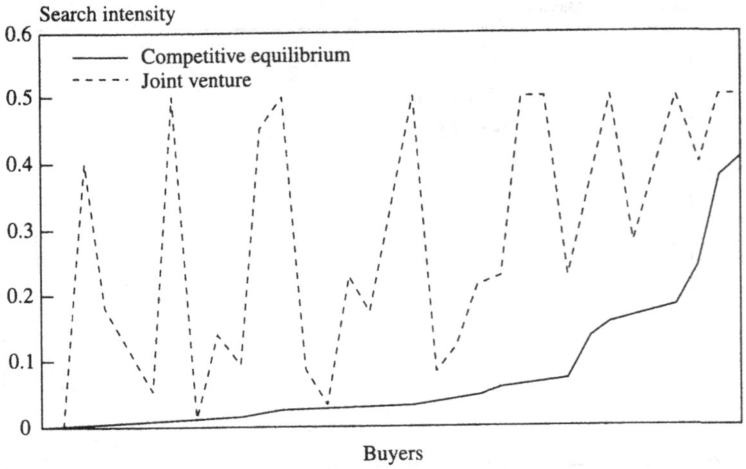

Source: Author's calculations, 2001.

Welfare Effects of a Broker's Presence in the Market

Although traders with a low level of search efficiency and high costs will always choose to use brokers if they are marginally better off doing so, their welfare increases in ordinal terms. However, traders who continue searching on their own lose welfare due to the arbitrary shrinking of the search market, and hence their expected payoffs from trade, over which they have no choice. As noted earlier, the positive or negative effect of brokerage on total welfare is not a general theoretical result, but rather an empirical outcome that is directly related to the distribution of search costs and of search efficiency in the market.

The results of the welfare analysis in the Ethiopian grain market using the actual distribution of search efficiency and search costs reveal that the presence of a broker increased the sum of net profits by 64 percent, from Eth. Birr 1,677 per transaction without brokerage to Eth. Birr 2,748 per transaction, or 13 percent of gross revenues. Figures 8.8 and 8.9 demonstrate the mixed welfare effects on individual sellers and buyers, respectively. A significant proportion of sellers, 47 percent, experienced welfare losses of 41 percent of net profits without brokerage, on average, while 61 percent of buyers experienced losses of 62 percent of net profits without brokerage, on average. However, these losses were compensated by the large gains experienced by the remaining 53 percent of sellers and 39 percent of buyers, who gained an average of 206 percent and 232 percent of their profits, respectively without brokerage.

The relationship between the welfare effects of brokerage, search efficiency, and search costs is demonstrated in Table 8.2. The average search efficiency of sellers and buyers who experienced welfare losses is .33 and .19, respectively, compared to the substantially lower average search efficiency of those who gained of .19 for sellers and .14 for buyers.

Similarly, the average search labor and search capital costs of traders who experienced welfare losses were Eth. Birr 156 and Eth. Birr 116 for sellers and Eth. Birr 204 and Eth. Birr 152 for buyers, in contrast to the considerably higher costs of Eth. Birr 301 and Eth. Birr 225 for the labor and capital cost of sellers who gained welfare and of Eth. Birr 272 and Eth. Birr 203 for the labor and

Figure 8.6 Brokers' effect on sellers' search intensity under competitive equilibrium, 1996

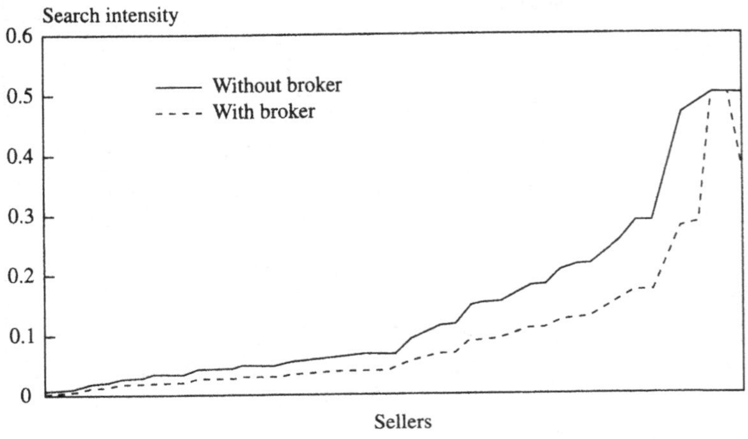

Source: Author's calculations, 2001.

Figure 8.7 Brokers' effect on buyers' search intensity under competitive equilibrium, 1996

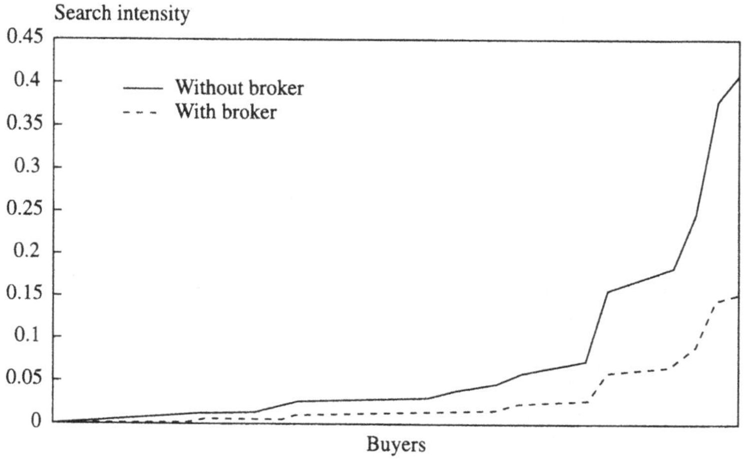

Source: Author's calculations, 2001.

Figure 8.8 Effect of brokers on sellers' surplus, 1996

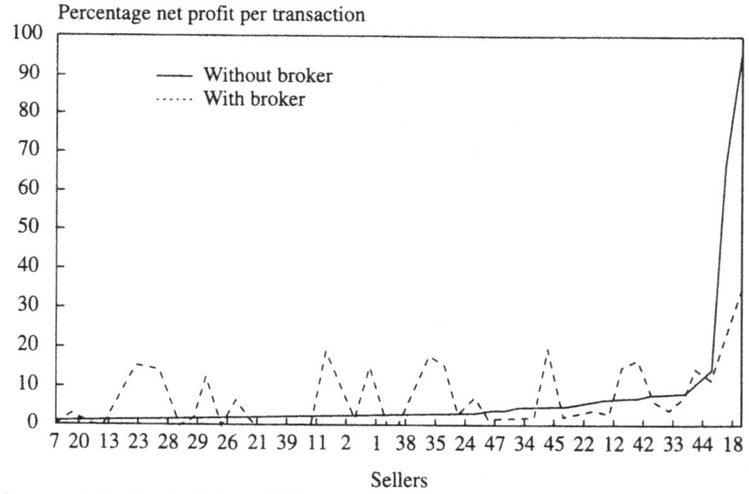

Source: Author's calculations, 2001.

capital costs of buyers who gained welfare from brokerage. Thus, the welfare effects of brokerage are conditioned upon each agent's specific search efficiency and search costs.

Socially Optimal Search with Brokerage

Although brokerage reduces the externality effect of individual search behavior, there continues to be a wide divergence between optimal search intensities with joint welfare under the competitive equilibrium model. The key difference between the two models is the addition of a second term in the first-order conditions for maximizing the joint welfare problem. This term adjusts the search intensity upward to take into account the effect of each agent's own probability of choosing a broker on the reduced payoff to the searching partner.

Figures 8.10 and 8.11 reveal that the divergence between the two models is more pronounced for buyers than for sellers, as noted in previous sections. It is interesting to note that the socially optimal solution results in an equilibrium level of 10 sellers and 10 buyers to the search market, where they optimally search at the maximum level of search intensity. In all cases, the socially efficient search intensity is higher than that in the competitive model. The first-order conditions for the joint welfare's problem imply that as the probability of the agent's own use of brokerage increases and the brokerage fee *jointly* increase, the socially optimal search intensities fall to the same level as the competitive economy.

The total economic surplus with brokerage is 60 percent higher in the joint welfare model than in the competitive model, increasing from Eth. Birr 2,747 to Eth. Birr 4,399. The joint welfare model with brokerage increases welfare 16 percent over the joint welfare model without brokerage. Table 8.3 provides a summary view of the welfare effects and the average optimal search intensities for each of the four alternative models discussed above.

Summary

This chapter has investigated the impact of the institution of brokerage on the optimal search behavior and welfare gains and losses of traders in the Ethiopian grain market. The theoretical expectations are broadly confirmed by the numerical data analysis.

The results suggest that without brokers, private search behavior in equilibrium widely diverges from the socially optimal strategies that would capture the positive spillovers of individual searches for trading partners. The presence of brokers appears to partially internalize this externality by forcing traders to make conjectures about the probability that potential trading partners may have switched to using brokers. The results show that with brokers there is less overall search intensity on the part of most individuals and that brokers in the economy have a positive effect on total surplus by enabling a more efficient allocation of search effort.

An important result from a policy perspective is that traders who were doing well without brokers stand to lose from the presence of brokers because of the shrinking of the search market that ensues. Thus, higher overall welfare is obtained at the expense of substantial losses by the relatively "search-efficient" members of the trader population. In the socially optimal model with brokerage, this welfare loss is avoided by maximizing the search intensity of those who search well while less efficient traders switch to using brokers. As a result, all traders are better off with brokers, and total surplus is 60 percent greater than in the competitive equilibrium with brokerage. The policy challenge facing Ethiopian policymakers then, and, more broadly, those concerned with strengthening market institutions in recently liberalized developing countries, is how to devise market policies that best achieve the socially optimal solution. In this context, policies must be devised that encourage the specialized function and search efficiency of brokers without adversely affecting the outcomes of relatively efficient traders. This could potentially be achieved by increasing the search efficiency of brokers relative to all traders so that all traders would gain from switching to brokerage and would not feel the adverse effects of the shrinking of the direct search market. Some policies that could enhance the specialized role of brokers would be the formalization of their role in the market (at present, brokers are not distinguished from traders in the eyes of the state), setting up rules of conduct and standards of entry for brokers (rules similar to those governing brokers on organized commodity exchanges), and strengthening their search capacity through training and improved access to market information and telecommunications.

Finally, although this study has revealed important insights regarding the implications of optimal search behavior and the heterogeneity of traders with respect to search costs and search efficiency, further research could be envisaged that extends the welfare implications to include the effects of market search behavior and the presence of brokers on producer and consumer welfare, in addition to that of traders.

Table 8.2 Welfare from brokerage, search efficiency, and search costs, 1996

	Welfare loss	Welfare gain
Sellers		
Percentage of traders	47 percent	53 percent
Average Birr amount (percentage of π)	41 percent	206 percent
Average search efficiency (γ)	.33	.21
Average labor costs of search (C_L)	155.89	300.84
Average capital costs of search (C_K)	116.40	224.63
Buyers		
Percentage of traders	61 percent	39 percent
Average Birr amount (percentage of π)	62 percent	232 percent
Average search efficiency (γ)	.19	.14
Average labor costs of search (C_L)	203.52	272.35
Average capital costs of search (C_K)	151.96	203.35

Source: Author's calculations, 2001.

Table 8.3 Summary of optimal search intensities and welfare effects of four search models

	Competitive equilibrium	Joint welfare
Without broker	$\Sigma^i\Pi_i + \Sigma^j\Pi_j =$ Eth. Birr 1,677 $S^* = .15$ $B^* = .08$	$\Pi^{SP} = \Sigma\pi_i + \Sigma\pi_j =$ Eth. Birr 3,798 $\bar{S}^*_{SP} = .28$ $\bar{B}^*_{SP} = .28$
With broker	$\Sigma^i\Pi_{,M} + \Sigma^j\Pi_{j,M} =$ Eth. Birr 2,748 $\bar{S}^{M*} = .10$ $\bar{B}^{M*} = .03$	$\Pi_M^{SP} = \Sigma^i\pi_{iM} + \Sigma^j\pi_{jM} =$ Eth. Birr 4,399 $\bar{S}^{M*}_{SP} = .24$ $\bar{B}^{M*}_{SP} = .26$

Source: Author's calculations, 2001.

Figure 8.9 Effect of brokers on buyers' surplus, 1996

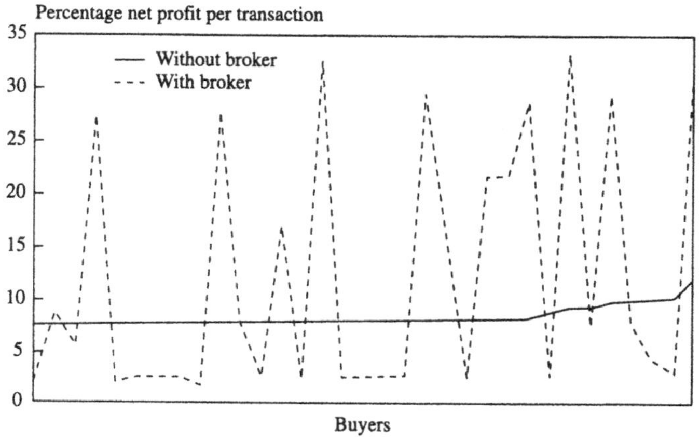

Source: Author's calculations, 2001.

Figure 8.10 Sellers' search behavior in competitive and joint welfare models, 1996

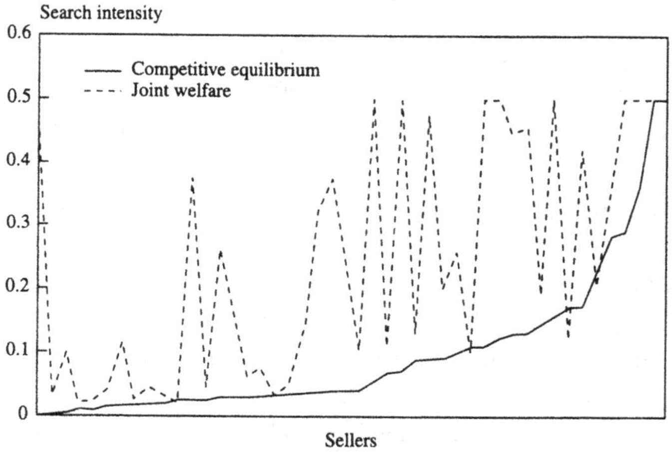

Source: Author's calculations, 2001.

Figure 8.11 Buyers' search behavior in competitive and joint welfare models, 1996

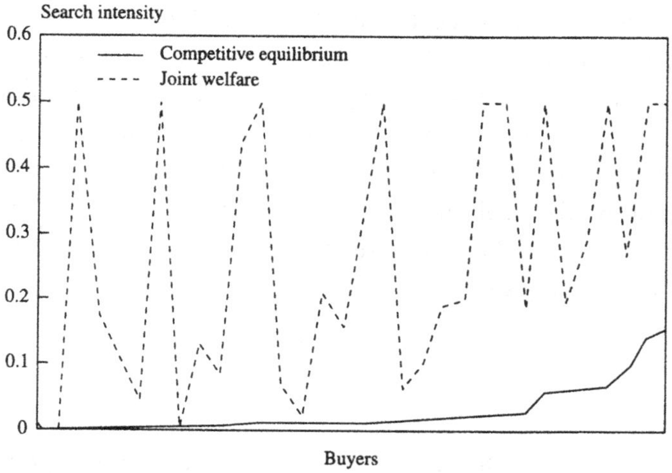

Source: Author's calculations, 2001.

CHAPTER 9

Conclusions and Policy Implications for Improving Market Performance

> Economic growth is dependent on stable political and economic institutions that provide low costs of transacting in impersonal political and economic markets.
>
> —Douglass North, 1989

With nearly half of the Ethiopian population dependent on the foodgrain market, the performance of the domestic market is vital for food security and economic growth. The liberalization of the Ethiopian grain market in 1990 has effectively reduced marketing margins and enhanced long-term market integration. Yet market performance remains "efficient but poor," to paraphrase Schultz's hypothesis, in that reform has not led to market development in areas such as contractual arrangements to transfer risk, increased impersonal exchange, the provision of value added beyond transport, and increased trader investments. A relatively low share of domestic production is marketed, 28 percent in a good harvest year such as 1995/96, and an even lower share goes through private marketing channels, only 18 percent of total production. Thus, the scope for increasing the scope of market participation both in volume and in value added remains high.

An important step in the design of appropriate market development policy is to better understand the links between market institutions, transaction costs, and the microeconomic behavior of traders. This study addresses a largely neglected area: *how* do buyers and sellers find each other in the market and at what cost? Using the New Institutional Economics framework, this study focuses on the institution of brokers, acting as intermediaries on behalf of traders, in the Ethiopian grain market. In addition to presenting new evidence on the arbitrage behavior of traders, this research report analyzes the nature and extent of transaction costs related to market search, the role of social capital, and the impact of the brokerage institution on minimizing search costs. The following findings are based on a national survey of wholesale traders and brokers conducted in Ethiopia in 1996.

Summary of Findings

Trader Arbitrage

Analysis of traders' operations and their arbitrage behavior reveals that Ethiopian grain wholesale operations are generally small-scale, personalized, enterprises in which the owner individually owns and manages the business. Social capital plays an important part in trade in that at least half of the traders interviewed are children of current or past traders, generally their fathers. Traders' arbitrage activity is mainly limited to transport, with an average distance of 200 kilometers for wholesale transactions. Overall, physical marketing costs related to transport, handling, and other costs represent 83 percent of gross margins. Traders' net margins are less than 5 percent of sale price, indicating that traders are quite competitive, particularly in the surplus region markets.

The Role of Brokers

Weak public market information, a lack of grain standardization, the oral nature of contracts, and limited legal enforcement of contracts are all factors that contribute to the difficulty that traders encounter in attempting to trade directly with unknown partners. In response to the risk of commitment failure, traders either choose to trade with partners with whom they have prior personalized relationships or they engage the services of a broker whose role is to conduct market searches on their behalf, inspect the grain delivered, handle the delivery and payment logistics, and guarantee the transactions. Brokers retain a repository of information on traders' market behavior and are thus able to deliver a very important good, trust, or *imnet*. The presence of brokers facilitates impersonal or anonymous market exchange between traders despite the constraints imposed by the market environment. Although 85 percent of the sample of traders indicated that they use brokers, the use of brokers remains somewhat limited. Overall, traders use brokers for roughly one-fourth of their transactions. For long-distance trade, traders use brokers for one-third to one-half of their transactions, suggesting that personalized exchange continues to be important.

A closer investigation of the norms and rules underlying agency relations between brokers and traders reveal that client relationships are generally long term in nature, with repeated interaction over an average of six years. A somewhat surprising result is that these relations are unrelated to ethnic ties; only 26 percent of traders have the same ethnicity as their brokers. Although traders have difficulty monitoring the actions of their brokers, they avoid conflict through established norms that provide incentive-compatible constraints on cheating by brokers. These norms include the specialization of brokers by region and the fact that a large number of traders in a given market all use the services of the same broker. These practices ensure that traders can inform each other of their broker's actions and collectively punish the broker in the event of cheating. Second, brokers are compensated with a flat fee rather than a percentage fee, which limits their incentive to incorrectly report the prices at which grain is transacted.

Transaction Costs of Search and Social Capital

Traders are constrained in terms of both the opportunity cost of market search labor and the opportunity cost of holding capital fixed during search. Traders spend between one and three days searching for potential buyers or sellers with whom to complete transactions. Many traders do not have other staff to conduct searches on their behalf, suggesting that the opportunity cost of their labor time is very high. Further indication of this is that traders estimate that, at the margin, an additional staff member would increase their operations by 47 percent.

Trader-specific transaction costs of search labor time and of holding working capital during search are estimated as shadow costs from the traders' profit functions, using instrumental variable estimation to avoid simultaneity bias. The results reveal considerable heterogeneity in transaction costs among traders and suggest that traders may be more capital constrained than time constrained.

Transaction costs are a significant share of the total set of costs, including physical marketing costs, representing 19 percent of total costs. However, traders in surplus and deficit markets diverge considerably, with transaction costs taking a higher share in the deficit markets, possibly because of the greater risk of commitment failure in purchasing grain of unknown quality. Thus, transaction costs might be more significant in trader's choice to use brokers in the case of distant purchases.

In addition, social capital, defined as the network of trading contacts available to each trader, is important in enabling traders to more readily find trading partners. Although traders invest in contacts in distant markets as well as in regular trading partners, ethnicity and kinship are not obvious factors in social capital. Thus, fewer than one-third of trading networks are based on common ethnic identity.

Brokers and Transaction Costs

An empirical model tests whether traders are individually rational in choosing to use brokers in order to minimize their transaction costs of search. Each trader's decision to use a broker is based on a two-tiered choice. First, traders decide where to trade, either locally or in distant markets. Second, they decide whether to use brokers for those transactions, based on their opportunity costs of labor and capital, their social capital, and their choices of location. The estimation results reveal that traders are individually rational in their choice of brokerage; the opportunity costs of labor and of capital had large and significant effects on the use of brokerage by the traders surveyed. Of the two costs, the opportunity cost of search labor had a larger effect in sales.

Brokers and Market Welfare

An optimal search intensity model is constructed in order to address whether the institution of brokers increases the global efficiency of the marketing system rather than just that of individual traders. The model supposes that individual search behavior has positive spillovers to other traders. The presence of brokers in the economy allows strategic interaction between the search decisions of market participants, because traders base their search decisions on conjectures about other traders' decisions to use brokers. With brokerage, traders with relatively higher levels of search efficiency and lower search costs choose to search on their own, while traders with low levels of search efficiency and high search costs choose to use brokers.

Numerical estimation of this model demonstrates that the presence of brokers increases total welfare by 60 percent. Traders with relatively high levels of search efficiency have small welfare losses because of the shrinking of the search market that results, while relatively inefficient traders have large welfare gains from using brokers.

Policy Implications

This study presents a comprehensive analysis of a key market institution, brokerage, and its links with transaction costs and social capital. The findings highlight how, in the context of the weak marketing environment of Ethiopia, the brokerage institution spontaneously minimizes transaction costs and facilitates exchange. However, the study also reveals that at present this institution plays a limited role in that traders continue to rely on personalized trade for a significant share of their transactions, even in distant markets.

In light of what has already been said, three areas of policy intervention emerge from the study findings. The first is addressing the constraints in the marketing environment that lead to high search costs. The second is reducing the dominance of personalized exchange, because it can limit the scope of the market and contribute to a reduced capacity to effectively respond to market signals. Related to this, is capitalizing on the welfare gains of brokerage through increasing the share of marketed grain handled by brokers.

Reducing the Transaction Costs of Search through a Grain Exchange

The key to reducing search costs is to reduce the average time required to find a trading partner for a wholesale transaction. At present, with or without a broker, it takes one to three days on average to find a trading partner, though it is important to bear in mind that the real issue is finding a partner that one can trust. The implications of this length of time are that traders incur the opportunity costs of both labor and capital in the form of grain inventory and working capital does not rotate as frequently as it could. Reducing search time would require the development of a means of readily informing traders and brokers of corresponding supply and demand while at the same time screening potential partners and maintaining records of traders' past behavior in the market. An organized grain exchange is a well-known mechanism that reduces search time, coordinates market offers, and effectively screens market actors. In a sense, the operations of the central market brokers described in this study resemble those of an informal grain exchange. Thus, a formalized institution such as a grain exchange, located in the central market of Addis Ababa, would leverage the role currently played by brokers, who would continue to carry out the matching function. If brokers were to operate in a formal exchange, their search efficiency would be enhanced through the use of information technology and improved logistical coordination of supply and demand offers.

At present, the central market of Addis Ababa plays a key role as a clearinghouse for grain supply and demand, serving all regions of the country. In addition to enjoying the presence of brokers who are specialized in market search and price discovery, Addis Ababa has a natural advantage in that it is located at the hub of the surplus zones (in the western, southern, and northwestern regions) and the deficit zones (in the eastern, northeastern, and northern regions). The radial structure of major road links and of telecommunications gives the Addis Ababa market an infrastructural advantage.

A viable exchange depends on a number of supporting institutions. Among these are a regulatory apparatus to establish rules and guidelines governing the behavior of buyers, sellers, and intermediaries on the exchange. Complementary are the legal underpinnings of an exchange, that is, commercial laws that address the conduct of the market. At present, the commercial code in Ethiopia is an antiquated French code dating to the 1930s, which has little relevance to the present actual trade practices. Third, a transparent system of grades and standards for different qualities of grains is required to ensure that transactions relate to clearly established norms. A corollary is the need for a neutral inspection service to ensure that traded grains fall within the established norms. Finally, a liquid grain exchange critically depends on a functioning system of trade finance. That is, an underlying warehouse receipt system that is closely supported by the banking institutions is needed to ensure the smooth transfer of payments across market actors. Other important elements for the functioning of an exchange include standardized contracts that incorporate standard contractual parameters such as dispute settlement, weight and quality tolerance, and force majeure provisions as well as a market information system.

Depersonalizing Personalized Exchange

This study indicates that traders avoid transaction risk in long-distance trade by trading with partners they know. Social capital, defined in both quantitative and qualitative terms as the number of trustworthy trading contacts, enables traders to carry out long-distance transactions given existing transaction costs. Thus, in addition to reducing search costs, a complementary policy is to target ways to increase traders' social capital. That is, if social capital relies on whom traders know, how do they get to know more? One means of expanding social capital is to change the way in which it is acquired. Social scientists distinguish "in-born" social capital from acquired social capital. In-born social capital is obtained as a right of birth into a particular ethnicity, religion, or family. Although this kind of social capital can be lost, it is difficult to acquire, since the acquisition does not depend on one's own actions.

Acquired social capital is obtained through one's own merit, over time, through repeated interaction, common interests, location, or various types of behavior. The policy challenge is to increase the relative importance or worth of the latter type of social capital versus in-born social capital. This can be done through the promotion of institutions such as trader associations whose membership is merit based and can be revoked depending on behavior. Similarly, existing licensing bureaus could be given the role of maintaining historical records of previous trade disputes and providing this information on request, offering services much like those of a credit reporting agency.

Increasing the Use of Brokers

This study shows that, despite the specialized functions of brokers in the market and the clear efficiency gains of using them, traders use brokers for only 25 percent of their total transactions. Even for long-distance transactions, where search costs are higher, traders use brokers for only roughly 33 percent to 55 percent of transactions and brokers handle only 16 percent of the total marketed surplus of grain. Although this may justify promoting direct exchange through expanding social capital, ultimately this strategy alone is not likely to expand the reach of markets sufficiently. Moreover, the specialized function of brokers in both matchmaking and price discovery is an important source of efficiency gains that would not be captured by expanding social capital. Thus, an important policy question is this: What constraints are there on traders' use of brokers?

A close examination of the relationship between traders and brokers reveals that traders have difficulty monitoring their brokers' actions and that mistrust and ensuing conflict are issues. Information asymmetry gives brokers more market power than individual traders. To get around this, traders work exclusively with the same broker for long periods, relying on trust-based relations, and work jointly with the same broker, using reputation as a disincentive to cheating by the broker. Thus, policy aimed at capturing greater market efficiency from increasing the use of brokerage services should address means of making the brokers' role more transparent and regulating their function in the market. To begin with, existing trade regulations do not distinguish brokers from other traders in the market by issuing brokers' licenses versus trading licenses. Policy to enhance the use of brokers could also address enforcement of the norms already established for this institution, such as the prohibition of brokers' buying and selling on their own account.[37] Policies to regulate brokers' market behavior could include policies regarding maintaining a record of past violations as well as a certification process for brokers.

In sum, the policy implications of this study are threefold. Within the existing market environment, policy can expand access to social capital and promote the use of brokers. At a more fundamental level, policy needs to address how to transform the marketing environment and effectively reduce search costs through a viable grain exchange. Establishment of such an exchange will involve a broad effort to first establish the various supporting institutions that are needed to truly change the context of markets in Ethiopia. These three policy recommendations should be viewed as complementary and mutually reinforcing, with the broad objective of expanding marketed surplus and making markets more functional relative to the needs of the population.

Lessons for Other Countries

This study contributes to the policy dialogue on the appropriate role of policy in liberalized markets in supporting market development. The study develops an innovative approach to measuring the transaction costs

[37] In many organized exchanges, brokerage houses are prohibited from taking advantage of their knowledge of their clients' orders to take a market position, a practice which is called "frontrunning."

of search and rigorously analyzing the effect of the institution of brokerage on minimizing search costs and on global economic efficiency. It also develops conceptual links between social capital and search behavior. The methodology used here can be viewed as an international public good that is broadly applicable to other market contexts where search is important and in which intermediaries play a particular market role. More generally, one of the insights that comes from this research is that policymakers need to directly address search as a key market issue that fundamentally influences market dynamics and the structure of the market. Second, transaction costs cannot be assumed to be uniform across market participants. Heterogeneity in individual transaction costs leads to different behaviors and different sets of institutions in the market. More important, heterogeneity implies that market-enhancing policies will have different effects on specific actors. Thus, in Ethiopia the proposed policies to reduce costs, to expand social capital, and to promote brokers will have some positive and some negative effects, which will need to be factored in during policy design.

References

Abbot, John, ed. 1993. *Agricultural and food marketing in developing countries: Selected readings.* Oxon, U.K.: Centre for Agriculture and Biosciences International.

Aitken, M., G. Garvey, and P. Swan. 1995. How brokers facilitate trade for long-term clients in competitive securities markets. *Journal of Business* 68 (1): 1–33.

Akerlof, George. 1990. The economics of caste and the rat race and other woeful tales. *Quarterly Journal of Economics:* 599–617.

Alchian, A., and H. Demsetz. 1972. Production, information costs, and economic organization. *American Economic Review* 62 (5): 777–795.

Alexander, Carol, and John Wyeth. 1994. Cointegration and market integration: An application to the Indonesian rice market. *Journal of Development Studies* 30 (2): 303–328.

Alvarez, F. 1881. *Narrative of the Portuguese Embassy to Abyssinia during the years 1520–1527, edited by Lord Stanley of Alderley.* Cited in Pankhurst (1961).

Amha, W. 1994. *Food grain marketing development in Ethiopia after the market reform 1990: A case study of Alabo Siraro District.* Berlin: Verlag Köster.

Amselle, J.-L. 1969. Rapport de mission sur l'economie marchande au Mali. *Cahiers d'Etudes Africaines* 9: 313–317.

Aoki, M. 1984. *The cooperative game theory of the firm.* Oxford: Clarendon.

———. 1998. Norms and other governance institutions. Stanford, Calif.: Stanford University. Mimeo.

Bardhan, P. 1989. Alternative approaches to the theory of institutions in economic development. In *The economic theory of agrarian institutions,* ed. P. Bardhan. Oxford: Clarendon.

Barr, A. M. 1997. *Social capital and technical information in the Ghanaian manufacturing sector.* Center for the Study of African Economies, Oxford, Oxford University, May. Mimeo.

Barrett, C. 1997. Food marketing liberalization and trader entry: Evidence from Madagascar. *World Development* 25 (5): 763–777.

Baulch, Robert. 1997. Testing for food market integration revisited. *Journal of Development Studies* 33 (4): 512–534.

Baye, M., and T. Cosimano. 1990. Choosing sides in matching games: Nash equilibria and comparative statics. *Economica* 57 (227): 283–293.

Bell, Clive. 1989. A comparison of prinicipal-agent and bargaining solutions: The case of tenancy contracts. In *The economic theory of agrarian institutions,* ed. P. Bardhan. Oxford: Clarendon.

Bereket, K., T. Jayne, and M. Tadesse. 1996. Urban grain consumption patterns in Ethiopia: Implications for food pricing policy and food aid programs. Department of Economics, Addis Ababa University, Addis Ababa, Ethiopia. Mimeo.

Berry, S. 1993. *No condition is permanent: The social dynamics of agrarian change in sub-Saharan Africa.* Madison: University of Wisconsin Press.

Beynon, Jonathan, S. Jones, and S. Yao. 1992. Market reform and private trade in eastern and southern Africa. *Food Policy* 17 (6): 399–408.

Bryceson, D. 1993. *Liberalizing Tanzania's food trade: Public and private faces of urban marketing policy 1939–88.* Geneva: United Nations Research Institute for Social Development.

Burdett, K., and M. O'Hara. 1987. Building blocks: An introduction to block trading. *Journal of Banking and Finance* 11 (August).

Central Statistical Authority. 1995. *Agricultural sample survey: Results of 1995/96 area, yield, and production survey.* Addis Ababa, Ethiopia.

Cheung, Steven. 1968. Private property rights and sharecropping. *Journal of Political Economy* 76: 107–122.

———. 1969. *The theory of share tenancy.* Chicago: University of Chicago Press.

Chicago Board of Trade. 1888. *Thirtieth annual report of the trade and commerce of Chicago for the year ended December 31, 1887.* Chicago: Knight and Leonard.

———. 1989. *Commodity trading manual.*

Clay, D., D. Molla, and D. Habtewold. 1998. Food aid targeting in Ethiopia: A study of household food insecurity and food aid distributions. Working Paper 12. Grain Market Research Project, Addis Ababa, Ethiopia.

Clay, K. 1993. Trade, institutions, and the law: The experience of Mexican California. Stanford University, Stanford, Calif. Mimeo.

Coase, R. 1937. The nature of the firm. *Economica* 4 (16): 386–405.

Cohen, A. 1969. *Custom and politics in urban Africa: A study of Hausa migrants in Yoruba towns.* Berkeley: University of California Press.

Coleman, J. S. 1988. Social capital in the creation of human capital. *American Journal of Sociology* 94 (Supplement): S95–S120.

Cosimano, Thomas. 1996. Intermediation. *Economica* 63 (249): 131–143.

Coulter, Jonathan, and P. Golob. 1992. Cereal market liberalization in Tanzania. *Food Policy* 17 (6): 420–430.

Cronon, W. 1991. *Nature's metropolis.* New York: W. W. Norton.

Dadi, L., A. Negassa, and S. Franzel. 1992. Marketing maize and teff in western Ethiopia: Implications for policies following market liberalization. *Food Policy* 17 (3): 201–213.

Demsetz, H. 1968. The cost of transacting. *Quarterly Journal of Economics* 82 (1): 33–53.

Dercon, S. 1995. On market integration and liberalisation: Method and application to Ethiopia. *Journal of Development Studies* 32 (1): 112–143.

Diamond, Peter. 1981. Mobility costs, frictional unemployment, and efficiency. *Journal of Political Economy* 89 (4).

Eswaran, M., and A. Kotwal. 1985. A theory of contractual structure in agriculture. *American Economic Review* 75 (3): 352–367.

Ethiopian Grain Trade Enterprise. 1996. *Statistical Bulletin* No. 4. Addis Ababa, Ethiopia.

Evers, H.-D., and H. Schrader, eds. 1994. *The moral economy of trade.* London: Routledge.

Fafchamps, Marcel. 1992a. Solidarity networks in pre-industrial societies: Rational peasants with a moral economy. *Economic Development and Cultural Change* 41 (1): 147–174.

———. 1992b. Non-convex transaction costs, networks, and market power. Stanford University, Stanford, Calif. Mimeo.

———. 1996a. Market emergence, trust, and reputation. Stanford University, Stanford, Calif. Mimeo.

———. 1996b. The enforcement of commercial contracts in Ghana. *World Development* 24 (3): 427–448.

Fafchamps, M., and B. Minten. 1999. Returns to social capital among traders. IFPRI MSSD Discussion Paper No. 23. International Food Policy Research Institute, Washington, D.C.

Feige, Edgar L. 1990. Defining and estimating underground and informal economies: The New Institutional Economics approach. *World Development* 18 (7).

Fisseha, T. 1994. Grain markets: Government intervention and liberalisation. Paper presented to the Fourth Annual Conference on the Ethiopian Economy, 28–29 November, Debre Zeit, Ethiopia.

Food Studies Group. 1992. *Study of the impact of the liberalization of smallholder produce marketing in Malawi.* Oxford.

Franzel, Steven, Forrest Colbur, and Getahun Degu. 1989. Grain marketing regulations: Impact on peasant production in Ethiopia. *Food Policy* 14 (5): 347–358.

Fukuyama, F. 1995. Social capital and the global economy. *Foreign Affairs* 74 (5): 89–103.

Gabre-Madhin, E., M. Fafchamps, R. Kachule, B. Soule, and Z. Khan. 2001. *Impact of agricultural market reforms on smallholder farmers in Benin and Malawi.* IFPRI Final Report, volume 2. Washington, D.C.: International Food Policy Research Institute.

Gebremeskel, D., T. S. Jayne, and J. D. Shaffer. 1998. *Market structure, conduct, and performance: Constraints on performance of Ethiopian grain markets.* Working Paper No. 8. Grain Marketing Research Project, Addis Ababa, Ethiopia.

Geertz, Clifford. 1968. The bazaar economy: Information and search in peasant marketing. *American Economic Review* 68 (2): 28–32.

Gibson-Jarvie, R. 1983. *The London metal exchange: A commodity market.* New York: Nichols.

Gilbert, E. 1969. *Marketing of staple crops in northern Nigeria.* Ph.D. diss., Stanford University, Stanford, Calif.

Goletti, Francesco. 1994. *The changing public role in a rice economy approaching self-sufficiency: The case of Bangladesh.* IFPRI Research Report No. 98. Washington, D.C.: International Food Policy Research Institute.

Grain Market Research Project. 1996. *Market information bulletin.* Ministry of Economic Development and Cooperation, Addis Ababa, Ethiopia.

Granovetter, M. 1985. Economic action and social structure: The problem of embeddedness. *American Journal of Sociology* 91 (3): 481–510.

Greene, W. 1993. *Econometric Analysis,* 2nd ed. New York: Macmillan.

Greif, Avner. 1989. Reputation and coalitions in medieval trade: Evidence on the Maghribi traders. *Journal of Economic History* 49 (4): 857–882.

———. 1993. Contract enforceability and economic institutions in early trade: The Maghribi traders' coalition. *American Economic Review* 83 (3): 525–548.

Hallagan, W. 1978. Self-selection by contractual choice and the theory of sharecropping. *Bell Journal of Economics* 9 (2): 344–354.

Hayami, Yujiro, and Toshihiko Kawagoe. 1993. *The agrarian origins of commerce and industry.* New York: St. Martin's.

Hayami, Yujiro, and Keijiro Otsuka. 1993. *The economics of contractual choice: An agrarian perspective.* Oxford: Clarendon.

Hayek, F. A. 1945. The use of knowledge in society. *American Economic Review* 35 (4): 519–530.

Heytens, Paul. 1986. Testing market integration. *Food Research Institute Studies* 20 (1): 25–40.

Hill, P. 1966. Landlords and brokers: A West African trading system. *Cahiers d'Etudes Africaines* 6: 349–366.

Hirschleifer, Jack. 1973. Exchange theory: The missing chapter. *Western Economic Journal* 11 (June): 129–146.

Hoff, K., and J. Stiglitz. 1990. Introduction: Imperfect information and rural credit markets: Puzzles and policy perspectives. *World Bank Economic Review* 4 (3): 235–250.

International Fertilizer Development Centre. 1993. *Ethiopian fertilizer and transport sector assessment.* Addis Ababa, Ethiopia: United States Agency for International Development.

Jackson, R. 1978. Nineteenth century market systems in Ethiopia and Madagascar. In *Marketplace trade: Periodic markets, hawkers, and traders in Africa, Asia, and Latin America,* ed. R. Smith. Vancouver: Centre for Transportation Studies.

Jayne, T. S., M. Mukumbu, M. Chisvo, D. Tschirley, M. Weber, B. Zulu, L. Johansson, P. Santos, and P. Soroko. 1999. Successes and challenges of food market reform: Experiences from Kenya, Mozambique, Zambia, and Zimbabwe. MSU International Development Working Paper No. 72. Michigan State University, East Lansing.

Jayne, T. S., A. Negassa, and R. Myers. 1998. The effect of liberalization on grain prices and marketing margins in Ethiopia. MSU International Development Working Paper No. 68. Michigan State University, East Lansing.

Jones, Stephen. 1996. Food markets in developing countries: What do we know? Working Paper No. 8. Oxford Food Studies Group, Oxford.

Jones, W. O. 1972. *Marketing staple food crops in tropical Africa.* Ithaca, N.Y.: Cornell University Press.

Kandori, M. 1992. Social norms and community enforcement. *Review of Economic Studies* 59 (1): 63–80.

Kherallah, M., C. Delgado, E. Gabre-Madhin, N. Minot, and M. Johnson. 2000. Agricultural market reforms in sub-Saharan Africa: A synthesis of research findings. Draft manuscript. International Food Policy Research Institute, Washington, D.C.

Kranton, Rachel. 1996. Reciprocal exchange: A self-sustaining system. *American Economic Review* 86 (4): 830–851.

Kuawab Business Consultants. 1994. *Structure of the Ethiopian grain market: A rapid appraisal.* Addis Ababa, Ethiopia: United States Agency for International Development.

Kumar, Shubh. 1994. *Adoption of hybrid maize in Zambia: Effects on gender roles, food consumption, and nutrition.* IFPRI Research Report No. 100. Washington, D.C.: International Food Policy Research Institute.

Landa, Janet. 1994. *Trust, ethnicity, and identity: Beyond the New Institutional Economics of ethnic trading networks, contract law, and gift exchange.* Ann Arbor: University of Michigan Press.

Lele, U. 1971. *Food grain marketing in India.* Ithaca, N.Y.: Cornell University Press.

Lirenso, A. 1993. Grain marketing reform in Ethiopia. Ph.D. diss., University of East Anglia, Norwich, U.K.

McCall, John. 1979. Economics of information and job search. *Quarterly Journal of Economics* 84 (1).

McDonald, J., and R. Moffitt. 1980. The uses of Tobit analysis. *Review of Economics and Statistics* 62 (2): 318–321.

Meillassoux, C. 1971. *The development of indigenous trade and markets in west Africa.* Oxford: Oxford University Press.

Menkoff, T. 1994. Trade routes, trust, and tactics: Chinese traders in Singapore. Cited in Evers and Schrader (1994).

Milgrom, P., D. North, and B. Weingast. 1990. The role of institutions in the revival of trade: The Law Merchant, private judges, and the Champagne fairs. *Economics and Politics* 2 (1): 1–23.

Mintz, Sidney. 1961. Pratik: Haitian personal economic relationships. In *Proceedings of the 1961 annual spring meeting of the American Ethnological Society.* Seattle: University of Washington Press.

Montgomery, J. D. 1991. Social networks and labor-market outcomes: Toward an economic analysis. *American Economic Review* 81 (5): 1408–1418.

Mooney, C. Z., and R. P. Duval. 1993. *Bootstrapping: A non-parametric approach to statistical inference.* Newbury Park, Calif.: Sage.

Mortenson, Dale. 1982. The matching process as a non-cooperative game. In *Economics of information and uncertainty,* ed. John McCall. Chicago: University of Chicago Press.

Mundlak, Y. 1996. Production function estimation: Reviving the primal. *Econometrica* 64 (2): 431–438.

Nabli, Mustapha K., and Jeffrey Nugent. 1989. The New Institutional Economics and its applicability to development. *World Development* 17 (9).

Narayan, D., and L. Pritchett. 1996. Cents and sociability: Household income and social capital in rural Tanzania. Policy Research Department, World Bank, Washington, D.C. Mimeo.

Natural Resources Institute. 1994. Food security in Ethiopia and the role of the Emergency Food Security Reserve Administration. Overseas Development Administration, Chatham, U.K. Mimeo.

Negassa, A. 1998. Vertical and spatial integration of grain markets in Ethiopia: Implications for grain market and food security policies. Working Paper No. 9. Grain Marketing Research Project, Addis Ababa, Ethiopia.

Negassa, A., and T. S. Jayne. 1997. The response of Ethiopian grain markets to liberalization. Working Paper No. 6. Grain Marketing Research Project, Addis Ababa, Ethiopia.

Newbery, David, and Joseph Stiglitz. 1979. Sharecropping, risk-sharing, and the importance of imperfect competition. In *Risk, uncertainty, and agricultural development,* ed. J. Roumasset, Jean-Marc Boussard, and Inderjit Singh. Laguna, Philippines: Agricultural Development Council.

North, Douglass C. 1989. Institutions and economic growth: An historical introduction. *World Development* 9 (September): 1319–1332.

———. 1990. *Institutions, institutional change and economic performance.* Cambridge: Cambridge University Press.

North, Douglass C., and R. Thomas. 1973. *The rise of the Western world: A new economic history.* Cambridge: Cambridge University Press.

North, Douglass C., and John Wallis. 1987. *Measuring the transaction sector in the American economy in long-term factors in American economic growth.* Chicago: University of Chicago Press.

Norton, Seth. 1992. Transaction costs, telecommunications, and the microeconomics of macroeconomic growth. *Economic Development and Cultural Change* 41 (1): 175–196.

Palaskas, T. B., and B. Harriss-White. 1993. Testing market integration: New approaches with case material from the West Bengal food economy. *Journal of Development Studies* 30 (1): 1–57.

Pankhurst, R. 1961. *An introduction to the economic history of Ethiopia.* London: Lalibela House.

Platteau, J.-P. 1994a. Behind the market stage where real societies exist, Part 1: The role of public and private order institutions. *Journal of Development Studies* 30 (3): 533–577.

———. 1994b. Behind the market stage where real societies exist, Part 2: The role of moral norms. *Journal of Development Studies* 30 (4): 753–815.

Plattner, S. 1989. Economic behavior in markets. In *Economic anthropology,* ed. S. Plattner. Stanford, Calif.: Stanford University Press.

Polanyi, K. 1957. *Trade and market in the early empires.* New York: Free Press.

Putnam, R. D., R. Leonardi, and R. Y. Nanetti. 1993. *Making democracy work: Civic institution in modern Italy.* Princeton, N.J.: Princeton University Press.

Ravallion, Martin. 1986. Testing market integration. *American Journal of Agricultural Economics* 68 (1): 102–109.

Ravallion, Martin, and L. Dearden. 1988. Social security in a moral economy: An empirical analysis for Java. *Review of Economics and Statistics* 70 (1): 36–44.

Ray, Isha. 1997. A farming systems analysis of irrigation institutions. Ph.D. diss., Stanford University, Stanford, Calif.

Rubinstein, A., and A. Wolinsky. 1987. Middlemen. *Quarterly Journal of Economics* 102 (3): 581–593.

Sadoulet, E., and A. de Janvry. 1995. *Quantitative development policy analysis.* Baltimore, Md.: Johns Hopkins University Press.

Sargent, Thomas. 1987. *Dynamic macroeconomic theory.* Cambridge, Mass.: Harvard University Press.

Sattinger, Michael. 1995. Search and the efficient assignment of workers to jobs. *International Economic Review* 36 (2).

Schmid, A. Allan, and James Shaffer. 1964. Marketing in social perspective. In *Agricultural market analysis,* ed. Vernon L. Sorenson. East Lansing: Bureau of Business and Economic Research, Michigan State University.

Scott, G. J. 1985. *Markets, myths, and middlemen.* Lima: International Potato Center.

Singh, Nirvikar. 1989. Theories of sharecropping. In *The economic theory of agrarian Institutions,* ed. Pranab Bardhan. New York: Oxford University Press.

Stigler, George. 1961. The economics of information. *Journal of Political Economy* 69 (3).

Szanton, Maria. 1972. *Right to survive.* University Park: Pennsylvania State University Press.

Tadelis, Steven. 1998. What's in a name? Reputation as a tradable asset. Stanford University, Stanford, Calif. Mimeo.

Thomas, N. W. 1908. The market in African law and custom. *Journal of the Society of Comparative Legislation* 19: 90–106.

Timmer, C. Peter. 1987. *The corn economy of Indonesia.* Ithaca, N.Y.: Cornell University Press.

Townsend, Robert. 1978. Intermediation with costly bilateral exchange. *Review of Economic Studies* 55: 417–425.

Trager, Lillian. 1981. Customers and creditors: Variations in economic personalism in a Nigerian marketing system, *Ethnology* 20 (2): 133–146.

Williamson, Oliver. 1981. The economics of organization: The transaction cost approach. *American Journal of Sociology* 87 (November): 548–577.

———. 1985. *The economic institutions of capitalism.* New York: Free Press..

Yavas, A. 1992. Marketmakers versus matchmakers. *Journal of Financial Intermediation* 2 (1): 33–58.

———.1994. Middlemen in bilateral search markets. *Journal of Labor Economics* 12 (3).

Zeller, M., A. Ahmed, S. Babu, S. Broca, A. Diagne, and M. Sharma. 1996. Rural financial policies for food security of the poor: Methodologies for a multi-country research project. Food Consumption and Nutrition Division Discussion Paper No. 11. International Food Policy Research Institute, Washington, D.C.

Zusman, Pinhas. 1989. Peasants' risk aversion and the choice of marketing intermediaries and contracts: A bargaining theory of equilibrium marketing contracts. In *The economic theory of agrarian institutions,* ed. Pranab Bardhan. New York: Oxford University Press.

Made in the USA
Monee, IL
08 November 2026

67984626R00063